RETIREN BEGINNING

A Guide to Creating a Retirement Strategy

Daniel J. DeVerna

Imprint: Independently published
Printed in the United States of America
Published by Daniel J. DeVerna

www.devernaco.com

*Daniel J. DeVerna offers products and services using the following business names: DeVerna
& Co Financial LLC – insurance and financial services | Ameritas Investment Company,
LLC (AIC), Member FINRA/SIPC – securities and investments | Ameritas Advisory
Services (AAS) – investment advisory services. AIC and AAS are not affiliated with
DeVerna & Co Financial LLC or any other entity mentioned herein.*

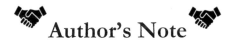 Author's Note

These days you cannot turn on the television or the radio and not be bombarded with advertisements for financial consultants promising everything from being your billiards buddy to claiming that they are somehow significantly different from the rest. Let me start by saying I do not have a dart board or pool table in my office, and in many ways, I am both different and yet the same as most of my competition. However, there are several notable differences that are important to understand.

So, to help you understand what makes my firm different, we must first cover the four phases of retirement planning. Phase one usually takes place when you are young or at least younger. It's the phase when you have come to the realization that it is in your best interest to seek the advice and services of a licensed and most importantly, an experienced financial consultant. During this phase your retirement date is most likely at a point off in the distance and the amount of investing you do grows alongside your income. Certainly, there are other factors, such as your risk tolerance and your typical happenings that everyone experiences at some point in life. When it comes to the latter, I'm referring to getting married, buying cars and houses, having children, and then taking the finances that come along with having a family into consideration.

Then there is phase two. Phase two is the crucial "telescope" phase. You are not quite at the point of digging the money up from the backyard and taking it to the casino, but you have your eye on it and you can see the horizon more clearly. During this phase a variety of factors will most likely influence you and I to make certain adjustments to your original plan based on where you are at in life at this point, who you are with on the journey, and most likely you will have a clearer idea of where you want to go.

Next, we have phase three. Phase three is what I call the "Pull the Lever" phase. Once you pull the proverbial lever, there is no turning back. You need to measure twice and cut once to take some verbiage from the world of carpentry. In most cases your income stops during this time. Usually because you are giving up your career and retiring. It may be a career that you have loved or not loved, you may be thrilled or sentimentally saddened, but either way the filling of the bucket comes to a halt. This means that some very crucial decisions need to be made. These decisions are based on math and law and advice from your financial consultant. Ultimately, the decisions are yours to make, but I assure you that you don't have to worry about making them alone. As your financial consultant it is my job to counsel you so that the best decisions based on your bucket, your math, the laws, and your wishes are made.

So, together we have figured out the nuances of your retirement. You have worked hard at filling your bucket, we have invested well, you have pulled all the right levers and have come to phase four.

Phase four is the "Legacy" stage. This is where we work together to see that all you have worked for and built up through smart investing, in other words, "your legacy" doesn't get snatched from your loved ones by the government, taxes, or other 'financial boogeymen" that dwell in the realm where the "should have planned for that" plans end up. Together we will make sure that your plans never see that abyss. We will do this by following the roadmap that I have established over my twenty-year career. A roadmap I know very well. We will work with attorneys, estate planners, accountants and others, utilizing the laws to work in your favor, so that your legacy wishes are safeguarded. We will make sure that your loved ones receive all that they can after you have passed on.

I wrote this book to help you better understand the complexities of retirement planning. Because as you already know, knowledge is power. Once you have read this book, you and I will be able to do much more together to ensure your financial well-being blooms in a safe and fruitful way. You will find information on the "Retirement Red Zone", what a dream retirement could look like, retirement destinations, what you should know about your plan, Social Security, healthcare, and so much more.

CONTENTS

RETIREMENT IS JUST THE
BEGINNING

Chapter One
Evolution

In 2016 I had an idea. I wanted a business card that would stand out. That would impress people at first glance. A five-dollar business card so to speak. I sampled different materials, like metal and wood, but nothing seemed to do the trick. Then my business coach suggested that I write a book. And that the book would, in the end, be my "five-dollar business card". At once I realized the potential of his suggestion, but I had never written a book before. The idea was daunting. Then I thought about my earliest days in the financial advisory business. Days where I put in overtime, stayed late, cold-calling potential clients in the hopes of building a book of business. These were tough times, full of doubt and rejection-where courage was only found in hunger, necessity, and the overwhelming need to take care of my young family. Those days would be my first real experience developing self-discipline-a quality that has served my clients, my business, and myself very well ever since. Little did I know that I was lighting the spark of what would be my evolution as a financial advisor and as a human being.

In the first version of this book, I titled the opening chapter 'Endurance' and I referenced Ernest Shackleton and his ship, *Endurance*. I spoke about being the metaphoric Navigator on a voyage of survival and exploration and used that parable to highlight the concept and importance of retirement planning.

About a year later, the first version of Retirement is Just the Beginning was published. That original book was written with Union workers in mind. It was pretty good for a first book. And from its pages, several more versions were born. Never to be one to let up on the gas, I kept writing. I published a book on retirement destination living and wrote numerous articles for magazines, published and eBook to help clients who had gone through or were going through divorce, and even have a couple of books that I have yet to publish. I guess you could say that I caught the writer's bug.

During this same period of time, in an effort to challenge myself on a personal level, I decided to venture out of the comfort and familiarity of my longtime Dojo, where I had been studying Kung Fu and Karate under Sensei Hurtsellers and try out something completely new. I needed a new challenge, so I started taking classes in Brazilian Jiu Jitsu, a martial art that, at least in practice, was completely foreign to me. It has proven to be a great decision. I still practice with Sensei Hurtsellers and I even teach classes there. But, by delving into BJJ, I forced myself to get out of my comfort zone once again, start at the bottom, both literally and figuratively, and embrace a form of humility that I had been lacking. Proudly, I had accomplished a lot at Sensei Hurtsellers' dojo. I gained valuable skills, knowledge of Bushido, or 'The Way of the Warrior', I passed tests, developed discipline, achieved higher and higher ranks, and what once were unfamiliar techniques, became second nature to me. Instinctually and without thought. But Brazilian Jiu Jitsu was a different animal. Remember that friend of mine with the smart-guy-itis? He told me once that chess was invented by an ancient Persian General to teach his commanders how to think strategically on the battlefield. To see your opponent's next move, to counter, and to think three moves ahead. In a sense, how to adapt to adversity.

BJJ is very much like the game of chess. It is just a physical version. You must anticipate your opponent's moves, look for openings in his guard, and plan your path to checkmate three moves ahead. And you must do this without rigid thinking, you must do this with the ability to change strategy without notice. It requires discipline, and conditioning, and most of all fluidity of thought. BJJ teaches lessons on and off the mat, every single day. For me, this has been extremely valuable as I have been able to apply these lessons, this way of adaptation to my business and my personal life. This would become another example of the "Evolution" that has taken place in my life since I published that first book.

I realized a long time ago that life comes at you hard and fast. And I'm sure that all of you have seen how the world has changed dramatically in just the past few years. How society has changed. How business, finance, and money have changed. Things that you probably never thought possible in your lifetime, both good and bad, have materialized into reality, into the new normal—and now we must all face the fact that what once was, no longer is, and tomorrow is going to be even more different. Benjamin Franklin famously quipped "Failing to plan is planning to fail." Those words resound with me now more than they ever have.

But the nature of retirement planning and wealth management has changed. There are new challenges, new influences, and most importantly new expectations. When I first started in this business, people who were retired or nearing retirement age were able to expect certain things to be true. There was a certain global pecking order. It was understood that the United States was the "top dog", the "American Dream" was almost a birthright, the banking institutions were solid, the markets were stable, Social Security was secure, and for many, pensions were something that was entitled.

You retired at 65, lived out your "golden years" basking in the fruits of a lifetime of diligent labor, and still were able to leave a legacy to the next generation. Retirement was pretty cut and dry. But if you've been paying attention, then you understand a lot has changed. A few years before I wrote the first version of this book, the unthinkable happened. After years of unchecked practices, the once solid housing market collapsed, sending the global economy into what was dubbed "The Great Recession". The markets tumbled, investment banks and insurance companies along with other businesses that were deemed "too big to fail " had to be bailed out by the Government with taxpayer dollars. It was the beginning of a new era, one in which things that had been taken for granted could no longer be. Sure, it created an opportunity for individuals and corporations alike, those that had the resources to weather the storm. All times of crisis create opportunities. But opportunities only exist if you can seize them at the right time, and in order to do so, you have to be able to spot the opportunity.

Luckily, my company, my clients, and myself, were able to weather the storm and seize upon the opportunities. This was due in part because for a long time, I have been investing in evolution. I regularly attend conferences with some of the sharpest economists, business leaders, innovators, and thinkers in the world today. Additionally, I keep my staff and colleagues aware that to keep our edge, we must remain nimble, up-to-speed with current trends and future forecasts, and always adapting, always evolving. Because, as I said earlier life comes at you hard and fast. Whether it's on the BJJ mats or in the global economy, you better be able to adjust your strategy on the fly, otherwise something is going to get broken.

So, I started the first book in 2016 and published it in 2017. Those were pretty good years. But some wild things were around the corner. I don't know about you, but I wasn't expecting the entire world to shut down because of a pandemic. But it did. Sure, we made it through, but it was tough at times, and it changed a lot of things. I know for me; it was another example of the necessity to expect the unexpected. To hope for the best, but to prepare for the worst. Sounds like a cliché, well, it is one, but that doesn't mean that it isn't true or wise. So, I continue my evolutionary path as both a human and a financial advisor. As a parent, a partner, and a friend. Look, there is a valid reason why I'm bothering to tell you all of this. It's because I want you to understand that I am aware that retirement is changing. What it means, what it looks like, how you get there, and of course, when you get there.

Unlike the majority of clients that were retiring when I first started my career, most of my clients today have different needs, desires, timelines, and ideas of what retirement looks like. The fact is that people are living longer and are more active. This requires a different strategy than the retirement plans of yesteryear. The price of admission to a "dream retirement" has increased in most cases, making it increasingly more important that the planning and the planners are evolving and adapting.

In the previous books, I spoke to the fact that nobody cares more about your money than you do. That fact remains true. I also spoke about how I used to get made fun of for saying that you had better "get the warm and fuzzy" feeling from your financial advisor. That fact also remains true. Whether you are a client of mine or someone else, you need to make sure that they have your best interest in mind. You need to make sure that your goals are clearly known and that there is a plan to achieve those goals that is not only realistic and timely, but also is nimble. A plan that can change in case an unknown or unforeseen situation develops. There was a time when investing was like cooking with a crock pot. You could just set it and forget it. But nowadays you want your "chef" paying close attention. The wrong ingredients or incorrect temperature so to speak, can spoil the meal.

A good portion of the first chapter in the original books was devoted to who I am and my story. As it was my first book, it made sense to tell you about me and to sell you on me. I hope that by now, we are more well acquainted. Many of you I have known for quite some time and a lot of you are friends. So, I will spare you the boasting and the biographical filler and leave it at this. I came from an honest and caring yet humble family upbringing. From them I learned the value of hard work and integrity. Those are two of my most guiding principles at work to this day. I have my own family, most of which are grown, but we are still a tight bunch. I'm proud of my children and I try to make sure that they remain proud of me. The business I founded has gone through some recent changes, but we have come out stronger because of them. I try to lead by example, treat my colleagues and staff with respect, and make sure that they have all of the resources and information to perform for our clients at 110% every day. And I understand if that ever changes, it will mean that it is time for me to pass the torch. In my professional life, my clients come first and always will.

In the pages that follow we are going to cover a lot of important topics. The goal of doing this is to help you prepare for your own retirement planning. Whether it's with me or someone on my team or someone completely unrelated to us, I can't stress enough the importance of hiring a professional financial advisor. There is an old saying, "You don't buy a dog and bark yourself." Your retirement needs deserve professional care and guidance. I drive to see clients regularly. In fact, I put a lot of miles on my Bronco. So, when it's time for a tune up or something needs to be fixed, I take it to a certified technician. I certainly don't try to fix it myself and I don't let just anyone work on it. Let's face it, you need to treat your financial health the same way, and when it comes time for managing your retirement, engage a professional.

Some of the information we are going to dive into are topics like the space and time leading up to pulling the retirement trigger. The necessity of a good plan and a competent planner and the importance of clearly defining your retirement goals and how you are going to get there. We are also going to look closely at the difference between 401 (k) and Roth IRAs as well as TRAP IRAs.

We'll examine healthcare needs and costs in retirement as well as life insurance and long-term care issues. There are sections on dream retirements in the modern world, retirement destinations both domestic and international, and alternative retirement lifestyle trends. Of course, Social Security and pensions will be covered along with early retirement packages, and everyone's favorite chapter about the value of having a relationship with a financial professional.

It remains true today that I still believe in looking someone in the eye and shaking their hand. As I've said before, I try to keep alive the old-fashioned values that my parents' and grandparents' generations believed in. And I still count my blessings and attribute much of my own success to this way of conducting business. I hope that you will appreciate it as well.

So, let's continue now with some examples of the most common questions that I have gotten in my many years as a financial consultant. I will expound on these in the chapters that follow in more detail, but for now here is a glimpse at what you can expect. You probably have already thought of most of these questions. But regardless, my purpose for this book is to help you understand the value of having a person like me work for you. As I mentioned earlier, you have worked hard for your money, and no one cares more about it than you. But dealing with the intricacies of managing it is probably not your purpose in life, what fulfills you, or frankly how you want to spend your time. It is, however, my purpose. So let me see if I can get you the warm fuzzy. Here goes:

1. WHEN CAN I AFFORD TO RETIRE?

This is a question I get a lot. And the answer for most people is growing ever more perplexing. Factors like multiple and complicated retirement plans, social security questions, and budgetary issues among employers muddy the already seemingly unclear waters.

The very decision to retire can be a source of stress because of the emotions that it brings up. The thought of leaving a work environment that has been such an important part of your life, as well as the colleagues and friends that you have spent so much time with, can be difficult.

Later in the book I will get into the nitty gritty of the details and cover all the bases. I will discuss things like how your age, financial circumstances, health, and family situation affects the decisions you will make. I will also talk about the timing of eligibility of collecting retirement benefits from your pension(s) or other sponsored retirement plans. We'll also examine some of the biggest factors involved in answering this question. Like, what kind of lifestyle would you like to have in retirement? Where would you like to retire? How long will your retirement last?

I'll try to keep your interest while answering these and other very serious questions and hopefully we might even have a little fun with it. After all, isn't retirement supposed to be fun? In my book, it is!

2. HOW WILL I PAY FOR HEALTHCARE IN RETIREMENT?

If you follow the news at all you know that healthcare is a hot topic. Health care seems to be ever changing. All the rhetoric about changing health care laws and entitlements can be scary. Pharmaceutical companies seem to pull the prices for drugs randomly out of a hat, and the costs just seem to increase. The same can be said about most other elements of the healthcare system. It is convoluted to say the least, elaborate in a best-case scenario, and downright frightening in a worst-case scenario. Knowing that health care will very likely make up a large proportion of your expenditures when retired makes planning for it crucial.

We will discuss issues like Medicare, employer sponsored benefits, out of pocket expenses, and home health aides. We'll talk about determining factors like age, health, and you and your spouse's family health history. We will use existing data and statistics and forecast as efficiently as possible future issues, costs, and trends. To put it mildly, it's kind of a big deal, so we'll take it seriously and give it everything we've got.

There is good news though. I make it a big part of my job to have the answers to this question and all the other questions about health care and retirement. I will go over some of the details further down the road in this book and assure you that there is a solution that makes sense to all the problems related to paying for health care in retirement. And I promise you that my team and I stay up to date so that your plans can adapt to whatever changes or obstacles come about.

3. WHAT SHOULD I KNOW ABOUT MY RETIREMENT PLAN?

This can be a daunting and confusing question, but don't worry. Although there are many types of retirement plans out there, there are also many readily available options. This book will outline many of them. Naturally, the best way to determine which plan is best suited for your needs is to meet with you personally, but after reading this book I believe you will come away with a better than basic knowledge of what to expect, what questions to ask, and how to proceed. I'll go over Defined Benefit (DB) Plans, Defined Contribution (DC) Plans, Hybrid Retirement Plans, and Supplemental Retirement Plans. It might seem complicated, but I'll break it down into easier to digest pieces. I promise that you will come away feeling informed and confident.

4. SHOULD I CONSIDER AN EARLY RETIREMENT PACKAGE?

The decision to accept a "buyout" or Early Retirement Package is complex. But guess what? I've got you covered.

These lump-sum distributions are usually based on your age, service, and contract. Whether or not to accept them or turn them down is different for everyone. Sometimes it makes financial sense. In some cases, you should turn them down.

We'll look at all the factors that need to be considered when deciding this matter. Issues like how early retirement will affect your pension benefits and other retirement income. When the appropriate time to start taking Social Security benefits is, does the buy-out come with low or no cost health care insurance until you are eligible for Medicare, and where you are at with your savings and investments will be covered in this chapter. We will examine the tax implications as well as the health of your employer in order to mitigate the risk of a future layoff. When all is said and done, you will be able to navigate this tough question with ease.

5. WHAT DOES A DREAM RETIREMENT LOOK LIKE?

Is relaxation, rocking chairs, and fishing with the grandkids your idea of retirement? Are you more likely to travel the world, ride across the country on your motorcycle, jump out of a perfectly good airplane, and start a new business? Maybe you like the idea of a bit of both.

Whatever the case may be for you, you've worked hard, and your dreams should be achievable. I'll help set you on the course to working towards whatever your dream retirement looks like. Further into this book, I'll discuss places to live in retirement where the dollar stretches further. Whether you're stretched out on a tropical beach, relaxing in a European hamlet, or living the dream right here in the U.S.A., I've done the research so that you don't have to.

6. HOW CAN A FINANCIAL CONSULTANT HELP ME?

Planning for retirement is like an expedition. Sometimes it may even seem more akin to a battle. And you wouldn't plan an exploratory trip to the South Pole or take on a hostile force without a strategy. A good financial consultant can help you strategize for your dream retirement. I do this by maximizing your income potential while managing your risk. This is partly accomplished by putting together a suitable plan for your retirement goals, smoothing over the process of the transition into retirement, and helping to make sure that your dream retirement is fully accomplished.

Through years of experience helping over 2000 households manage this process I've learned a lot. Most importantly, I've learned how to avoid the pitfalls that trap and misguide so many people in their retirement planning. But remember, it is my job as the professional to help guide you to reach your desired destination. And if you let me, I'll do just that.

Chapter Two
The Retirement Red Zone

If you've ever spent any amount of time at a pub somewhere in America, I'm sure you've overheard this conversation, "Who's the greatest quarterback of all time?"

Essentially, they're asking you to determine the best at football's most important position. Most folk's shortlist will mention Peyton Manning or Tom Brady. Or older players, from eras gone by consistently make the cut; players like Otto Graham, Unitas, Bradshaw, Elway, and Marino. But one name you'll almost always hear on this greatest-ever list is Joe Montana.

Why is that? Joe Montana's numbers aren't as great as others that are frequently listed. Not all of his statistics add up to supreme greatness. He never led the league in passing. He never had 4,000 passing yards in a season. What made Montana so great was that he played his best when it mattered most. In four Super Bowls, he had eleven touchdowns and zero interceptions. He won every Super Bowl he played in, and in three of them, was awarded most valuable player. When the game was on the line, when the pressure was at its peak, Joe Montana performed. It's how he got his nickname, Joe Cool.

In terms of your finances, you want your money to perform at its peak level when the pressure is the greatest. When is that? It's when you are near your retirement target date. In the NFL, they have an area of the field called the red zone. The red zone is when the offense drives the ball into their opponent's 20-yard line. It signifies that the offense is closing in on scoring points. And the red zone is precisely where you want your team to perform its best. The same goes for retirement planning. As you near your retirement date, as you reach your retirement red zone, you want your financial plans to score big for you.

The retirement red zone is mostly measured in the years before you plan on retiring, but there are some other factors which tell you that you are in the retirement red zone. To break it down as simply as possible, things get urgent within five to ten years of your retirement date. When you reach this point, you had better have a path defined. That is not to say that you can't still fix the mistakes of the past because in most instances you can. But it is to say that it is very important that your plan be entirely in place.

I'm not knocking anyone, especially hard-working seniors, but unless your ideal retirement is working as a greeter at Wal-Mart just to make ends meet, then you'd better not screw up once you hit the retirement red zone.

Not to worry though, telling the masses hello and goodbye whilst trying to tag returns can be avoided. And one of the ways to avoid having to do something that you might not necessarily want to do, is to ensure that the date you set for retirement is well thought out and appropriate for your unique financial situation.

Quitting your job may be high on your list of things to do, but let's do it for effect, not affect. That is to say, let's do it based on what it will accomplish, not just for the action of doing it. I hope you understand that this analogy is more than a grammar lesson. It is a crucial retirement planning lesson.

Another example of the retirement red zone's importance came in the crash of 2007/2008. Many people were heavily invested in traditional stocks and bonds, the value of which dropped to low levels during the recession. Those people who were not diversified properly had a very rude awakening. To say the least, they were caught off guard. To say it more plainly, they failed to have life's "what ifs" covered.

My solution to that involves being proactive, not reactive. It is about being aware that events like the one that took place in 2007/2008 and the systemic causes of it, can happen again, and suddenly. And the only way to ensure your money is in the safest possible harbor is to be fully engaged. There must be a plan to combat the proverbial "rainy day" or unforeseen circumstances that lead to an off market. This is, in part, accomplished by what I call having a "bucket" filled with low-risk investments.

Think of it like this: when that rainy day hits, imagine you're in your boat, safely floating in your harbor. Suddenly, the boat starts filling with water. That "bucket" will bail you out. Low risk investments can help keep you remaining afloat so that you can weather the storm.

So, we've covered the idea of what the retirement red zone is and what you can do to protect yourself from losing the game. We know that the red zone is when most people get serious about planning for retirement. But I don't think you can plan for retirement too early. The idea of mapping out each year and keeping your eye on the prize makes a lot of sense. After all, you don't want to panic before kickoff in the Super Bowl. If you don't have a plan, you'll find yourself scrambling. If you want to play it cool, it's crucial for people like yourself to have an educated opinion about retirement options. Let's huddle up a moment and draw a few plays. Let's develop a strategy so you feel comfortable with the retirement plan we have created.

But before we do that, let me call a timeout. What if I told you that you could retire at a much younger age if you were to put away just an extra hundred dollars a month? Would you do it? I always tell my younger clients the same thing. In the end, you will think one of two things: "I am glad I listened to Dan." or, "I wish I had listened to Dan." Let's make sure that you end up responding with the former and not the latter. Because, if your investments are symbolized by the quarterback in the retirement red zone, your financial consultant had better be a winning coach.

As a financial consultant focused on helping real folks like you, one of the most common questions I get is, "When can I afford to retire?" More than ever, retirees and pre-retirees in most careers have an added stress in retirement planning. Dealing with complex benefits packages and ever-changing options can really make planning for retirement stressful and a big whopping headache.

Don't worry though, I've got this covered, and soon you will too. There are some important things to keep in mind. For example, be thinking about the following ages: 55, 59 ½, 62, 67, and 73.

At 55, some plans allow for a person to have access to funds in some of their retirement plans. At 59 ½, most everyone has expanded options in their retirement plans, along with an option to draw on funds without penalty. At 62, most are eligible for Social Security, and each year that you don't take that out you get a potential pay raise for the future. At 67, you are at full Social Security retirement age and can receive benefits with no restrictions on income. And lastly, at 73, if you have not started taking money out of your qualified retirement accounts, you will have to, as the Government demands that you take required minimum distributions (RMDs).

In addition to being confusing and stressful, when and how to retire can be emotionally draining. You've spent a lifetime committed to working and helping others achieve their goals. It can be tough to think about yourself.

We, as Americans, build up this idea of retirement, but many have not taken the time to truly think about what that means. In some cases, it means sitting on the back porch smoking a cigar. In other cases, it means traveling the globe. Either way, you need to prepare for the transition from working to ensure that it is the happiest time of your life. This also is helpful in mapping out the budget through retirement, particularly from ages 55 to 75, where the income stream has to be the most resilient. Going from working full time to being without work can cause undue anxiety. Also, the realization that your previous job will continue without your efforts can be hard to take. With that said, having a plan that allows you to fulfill your purpose in this next chapter of your life will help alleviate some of those unneeded anxieties.

When you combine the financial questions and worries with the mixed emotions boiling inside you, it's no wonder so many people put off a retirement strategy until the very end.

It's okay to be fearful of retirement planning. Believe it or not, the average American is more fearful of losing their financial security than they are of death! That is why it is so utterly important that you find the right person to help with this daunting task. Someone who will unmask the boogey man and expose everything, right or wrong. Sure, it may be a scary thought to see behind the curtain, and you may feel that your personal situation is far worse than that of others but rest easy. The truth is there is no boogey man. Even the great and powerful Wizard of Oz was just a man with flashing lights and a loudspeaker.

Through it all, I can tell you this- I've had many people come into my office with what I call their financial junk drawer, turn it upside down and dump it all on my desk. Each time this happens, they end up sighing in relief afterwards and exclaiming that they wish that they had done it a long time ago. So, whether you are considering retirement soon or even if it is a long way off, I can tell you that it is time to have that chat.

You may not like to think about the possibility of unpleasant things happening in your life, but should they happen, they will be a lot more palatable if you have a plan for them. Things like a disability or even a death. With the proper plan, you can ensure that your family is taken care of. I know, for most people, that is very important, just as it is for me. Other unpleasant events, like an unforeseen divorce and/or having to move from your home, can also have a large impact if not planned for in advance.

Many of the measures that we use to help people decide when to retire are based on resources, and of course, desires. For instance, if you are like me and love your job, then the timeline is not as important as compared to someone who dislikes their work.

This is where I'll tell you about Al. Some years ago, I got a call from an almost frantic gentleman named Al. He worked for a major company that you would surely recognize, if named. Al was extremely frustrated at work. He had worked with stockbrokers and financial people before, but felt as though he had not found the right one. A client of mine, and a friend of his, told him that I would be the right guy to talk to. So, we scheduled some time to get together. This is when he gave me all of his information and dumped his proverbial financial junk drawer on my desk. This drawer had been compiled over 30 years. Then he asked if I would be able to give him a plan in which he would be able to retire…by the end of the month!

I went back to my team and crunched the numbers and ran Al and his family's situation through our process. A week later, I was sitting with Al and told him that he could retire at the end of the month. As you can guess, this was music to Al's ears. The thought of telling his employer that he would be retiring made him very happy, to say the least. The funny thing about the rest of this story is that Al worked for six more years. It seems that, once Al knew he had the power to walk away, it changed from something that he *had* to do to something that he *could* do. In his mind, something magical happened and work wasn't so bad after all.

So don't stress. With a few simple questions, you can know if you are on-track financially to meet your retirement goals. Here are a few considerations that can help you know if you have the potential to retire comfortably.

Question: Can I retire with Debt?

Yes. But there is a catch! The higher the debt, the greater your retirement expenses will be. Many Americans are retiring with high levels of debt.

Question: What are my projected retirement expenses?

This ranges from basic needs like housing and food, to lifestyle expenses like travel and entertainment.

Question: What sources of income do I have?

There's many: social security, benefits and pension, rental properties and part time work, are just a few of many.

Let's take a moment to look at these in greater detail.

Can I Retire With Debt?

In many instances, people retire with debts like mortgages, car payments, and maybe even student loans that they are paying on behalf of their children or grandchildren. Some debts even have tax advantages associated with them. With the right planning in place, retiring while carrying debt, although not ideal, can be managed and serviced without disrupting lifestyle.

What Are My Retirement Expenses?

Although there are some basic expenses that prove to be true across the board for all retirees, determining your expenses in retirement depends upon the individual and their choice of and level of lifestyle. Some factors that determine your expenses are: where you live, health care costs, what activities you partake in, and generally how "high on the hog" you choose to live. Other issues to consider when planning how to handle your expenses in retirement include provisions for unforeseen medical needs and long-term care issues.

What Sources of Income Do I Have?

Some retirees retire to a new career or another job. Some start businesses and have income from those ventures. Whether a new career or starting a business is in your future, many of you will have, in addition to Social Security, pensions and income from investments. Make sure to check out the chapters on Social Security and retirement investment plans later in this book.

The truth of the matter is that planning for retirement doesn't come with an easy-to-follow playbook. There is no simple formula that works for everyone. Unfortunately, when you find yourself in the red zone, there isn't much room for error. That doesn't mean that the sky is falling either. It just means that the main reason people always throw the keys to me, in the hopes of getting home in one piece, is because they know I have the knowledge and skills to help get them home.

When it comes to putting together a plan that makes sense for your individual needs, whatever they may be, I can promise you that I've done the research, helped a lot of people achieve the retirement of their dreams, and, next to you, am the person who cares most about your money.

Can I afford to retire checklist
How will I cover my healthcare needs? What are my planned budget and lifestyle expectations? What's my Social Security income? What are my pension plans? Do I have any potential inheritances? Have I considered my non-qualified assets? Do I have retirement plan assets? What are my other income sources? How much current debt do I have?

Consider This:
From the Desk of Dan DeVerna

In my practice, I am seeing more and more people retire early because of the effect that rising interest rates has had on lump sum payouts. In these scenarios, they gain the ability to do something that they want to do **rather than something that they have to do!**

Chapter Three
What Does My Dream Retirement Look Like?

In a multi-decade study, Harvard sociologist, Dr. Edward Banfield, sought to better understand why some people become wildly successful, while most did not. His research uncovered some surprising findings. Factors like intelligence, family background, and access to influential contacts had little to do with determining someone's success. What he discovered was that most successful people had a similar attitude. Most had the same frame of mind.

Dr. Banfield labeled this mindset the attitude of "longtime perspective." He concluded that the people who were the most successful in life were those who took a long-term outlook. People who took the future into consideration with each present-day decision were more likely to move up in life. By thinking of the future, they were more likely to endure present hardships and do the difficult tasks required to move ahead.

Thinking about that now, it makes perfect sense. When you have your eye on a prize, when there's a goal that you're fixed on, you're less likely to quit. A small bump in the road or patch of hard times are easier to endure when you are fixated on your destination.

With Dr. Banfield's long-term perspective in mind, let's think about your retirement. What does your dream retirement look like? Take a moment to relax. Picture yourself at ease. What kind of weather surrounds you? What are the sights, sounds, and smells that greet you as you watch the day pass? Are you alone? Are you spending more time with loved ones? Or maybe you're out exploring and enjoying your passions.

There is no right or wrong here. It's about you and what makes you happiest. Everyone's retirement dream is different. But it's more than just a dream. Thinking about what your perfect retirement looks like is an important exercise. Knowing what you want is a key aspect of strategizing your retirement planning. Why not take a moment to dream about it? It's only the rest of your life.

Perhaps you have pursuits that you have not yet had time to act upon. The dream of learning to play a musical instrument or maybe even to be in a band. Perhaps you desire to learn a new language or other type of skill. Some of you may even want to go back to school. Did you know that many universities offer free classes to seniors?

Maybe your dream retirement involves adventure and travel. To go off and explore. See the world. Relax on a beautiful beach in French Polynesia. Go on a wildlife safari in Africa. View the Northern Lights. Or, for those with a real wanderlust, maybe sailing around the world is your idea of a dream retirement.

For some of you, none of the aforementioned things will be on your personal bucket list. Instead, maybe your dream retirement is relaxing with family and friends. Spending more time with your spouse, children, or grandchildren. Maybe for you, taking it as easy as possible is the appropriate reward for a lifetime of hard work.

Whatever the case, it doesn't really matter as long as you have the plan in place to do whatever it is that you want to do. And guess what? With the right planning, you can even decide to have multiple dream retirement scenarios…perhaps a combination of globetrotting adventure and easy-going relaxation with the family.

My job is to help you be secure in your retirement. But your job is to figure out what your dream retirement looks like.

Let me give you three different scenarios from a recent business trip of mine to Florida's Gulf Coast.

For a long time, I had been promising to visit a client in Tampa. Finally, my schedule allowed me that opportunity. So, I flew down and figured that, while I was there, I would take the time to make some other visits.

I'm sure glad that I did. It was very gratifying to see individuals that I helped, living their versions of dream retirements. It was also eye opening. I'm happy that I can share these many different experiences with you now. Although they were all from the same trip to Florida, you will see that they showcase many very different situations.

Scenario One

How's this for a dream retirement scenario? My clients, Mike and Nikki, are closing on the sale of their dream boat, a Beneteau 473 sailing vessel. Soon, they will be embarking on their version of a dream retirement, sailing from the Gulf of Mexico to Florida, where they will be spending the holidays. After that, they are charting a course to the Bahamas to revisit some of their favorite spots, as well as explore some new locations in the archipelago. When the season ends in the Caribbean, they are making the crossing to the Mediterranean Sea. There, they will have the opportunity to visit ports from Spain to the Greek Isles. They will not be subject to any schedule, except for chasing the sun. Who knows, I may even meet up with them in one of my favorite spots, the French Riviera.

Scenario Two

Let's call this one 'The Tale of Two Retirements' in a nod to old Charles Dickens. My parents, Larry and Marje, were living a retirement scenario that I see playing out more and more. They were taking care of my grandfather, Ralph, who, although he lived independently up until he passed at the age of 98, still needed assistance. Having fought the Nazis in WWII, my grandpa was no stranger to fighting the good fight, but, like most people in their nineties, he needed some help with daily life, which my parents provided him with pleasure.

When my grandfather's time came and he passed away, my parents entered the second act of their retirement tale. Suddenly, their responsibilities decreased, their free time increased, and their finances were boosted by an inheritance. What this means to them is that they now have more options for traveling and checking off some of their own retirement wish list items. And the best part is that, whatever they decide to do can be done knowing that they were a big part of my grandpa getting to live independently in his own home, as we wanted.

As I mentioned, I see similar scenarios play out with more and more clients these days, as people are living longer.

Scenario Three

John and Tammy, two longtime clients of mine, decided to sell their home in Ohio and use their second home, a condo in Florida, as a base to do their version of a dream retirement.

They have four children who all have families of their own. John and Tammy decided that they wanted to spend a year living near each of their children and grandchildren. The interesting part to this plan is that one of their kids lives in Denver, Colorado, one lives in Seattle, Washington, one in Columbus, Ohio, and another in Nashville, Tennessee.

They are not only getting to spend some real quality time with their kids and grandkids, but they are also getting to experience some neat and different places while doing so.

Scenario Four

My clients, Paul and Samantha, chose to sell their family home in Toledo and reinvest the proceeds into a summer home on the water in Marblehead, Ohio and into a condo in Florida, where they can spend the winter.

Being that their children are grown up and have moved out, they no longer needed their big family home nor were factors like jobs or school districts of concern any longer.

They now get to spend summers when their grandchildren are out of school nearby at their lake house where, as a family, they can enjoy activities like boating, fishing, and other water sports.

Then, when Ohio winters set in, they get to go to their condo in Florida and enjoy sunshine and warm weather. Paul recently told me that the best part of having the winter location in Florida is that there is never a shortage of family and friends wanting to come visit.

Scenario Five

Got time for one last example of a dreamy retirement? Longtime clients of mine, Sherri and Robert, were able to retire from their teaching jobs in their mid-fifties. However, they wanted to keep working at something and eventually landed remote jobs as tutors. Working from a digital "location" gave them the freedom to sell their home and move to a "55 plus" retirement community in South Carolina.

This is not your grandparents' retirement community though. It's more like a cross between a country club and a resort. Since they are only working their remote jobs on a part-time, at-will basis, Sherri and Robert have plenty of time to enjoy all of the amenities and activities that come along with their new community.

I visited them and was blown away at some of the offerings from bars and restaurants to a wide range of sports and leisure choices. Literally, there is everything from pickleball to shooting ranges. The community also offers classes, clubs, and other group settings through which making new friends becomes very easy.

These types of communities are becoming ever more popular with retirees and are often in fun places with great climates, like the Carolinas where Sherri and Robert chose, as well as Florida, Texas, and Arizona to name a few other destinations. A while back, I wrote a book with a colleague that spoke about these places, and the response was tremendous. So, I decided to expand on the subject in this book and am looking forward to writing another book, going into even greater detail on the whole "destination retirement living" scene. So, stay tuned, readers!

I have numerous other examples, beyond the ones laid out here, that illustrate how today's retirees can plan on living long, full, and active lives after they retire. No longer is retirement a slow ride off into the sunset. Instead, you're starting an exciting new chapter of your life. With a little dreaming, and the right planning and investments, you, too, can redefine what retirement means.

It seems as though, here in America, we build up the idea of retirement, but often never get past the thinking stage. The question is, what would, or will you do in retirement? Whether it's today or five years from now, what do you want out of life? You need to put some real thought into what you would actually like your retirement to be like.

Let's go back to Dr. Banfield's long-time perspective for a minute. In doing so, I think you will be able to see that just knowing your retirement can truly be the fulfillment of a lifelong dream will make doing whatever it takes to get there a whole lot easier. Sure, there are components like planning, saving, and investing involved in making a dream retirement a reality, but if you were to ask anyone who is living theirs, I know that they would tell you that it's all worth it.

In the next two chapters, we will discuss places to retire should you be interested in living somewhere else. First, we will keep it close to home and talk about some great places to retire right here in the United States. Then, we will cast our net farther afield and look at some terrific places for retirement abroad.

In both chapters, we will touch on some of the advantages that certain locations offer. In discovering these factors, you just might find that your dream retirement involves packing up and moving. It isn't necessarily for everyone, but for some, it can change the whole dynamic of retirement.

What Does My Dream Retirement Look Like?

Does my dream retirement involve:

Can I afford to do what I want to do instead of what I must do?

Travel?

Adventure?

Learning?

Working at a new career?

Relaxing?

Spending time with loved ones?

Or something unique to me?

Chapter Four
IRA Versus Roth IRA.
401(k) Versus Roth 401(k)
What's the Difference?

What's a 401(k)?

Take a guess. Which section of the IRS tax code defines a 401(k)? If you guessed section 401(k), you are correct. That's where the strange name comes from.

At the basic level, a 401(k) is an employer-sponsored deferred contribution retirement plan. The way it works is simple enough. You elect to sign up for a 401(k) plan through your employer. Then you select the investment options that work best for you within the plan. Next, your workplace takes a portion of funds out of your paycheck before income taxes are withdrawn and deposits the amount in your plan. In some instances, as an added incentive, your 401(k) contributions are matched by your employer.

So, how do you get your money? Simple. When you reach retirement age, you take your money out of the 401(k)s. However, when you withdraw from your 401(k) that money is subject to income tax. Since you didn't pay taxes on those funds earlier, the IRS taxes you later when you withdraw. If you're paying taxes either way on the money, what's the big deal with 401(k)? When you defer your taxes until later down the road, the assumption is that you will be in a much lower tax bracket at retirement age than when you are in your prime earning years.

As it stands, there's no limit on the income level of a person who can contribute funds into a 401(k). But do keep in mind, as of 2022, there is a maximum that can be contributed between employee and employer in the same year. You'll have to stop at $61,000.

Features of a 401(k)

401(k) contributions often result in tax savings during the years with contributions.

Many employers offer to match a portion of your contributions.

Contributions can be taken directly out of your paycheck; this is an easy way to contribute without any work on the participant's part. Sort of out of sight, out of mind.

Compared to a Roth IRA, you can contribute more each calendar year with a 401(k).

What's a Roth IRA?

A Roth IRA is an individual retirement account you set up directly with an investment firm. Senator William Roth was the legislative sponsor of the individual retirement account, hence the name, Roth IRA.

Here's how they work. When you set up a Roth IRA, you work directly with a broker. After you create an account with them, you select the investment options you like and directly deposit after-tax funds into your Roth IRA.

After you've had the plan for more than five years and are over the age of 59 1/2 years old, you can withdraw all of your investment gains and deposits, tax frce. There are a few exceptions as well. For instance, you can use Roth IRA funds to put a down payment on a home or towards your child's tuition.

Like the 401(k), there are maximum contributions you can make to a Roth IRA. As of 2024, the maximum amount is $7,000 a year for anyone under the age of fifty or $8,000 for those over fifty. But, do keep in mind, there are income limits on who can contribute. For instance, if you earn $146,000 to $161,000 individually or $230,000 to $240,000 jointly, you are not allowed to contribute the full amount to a Roth IRA. In some cases, you may be excluded from any contributions.

In a sense, there is a bit of reverse discrimination going on here because, if you earn a higher income, you can be phased out of a Roth IRA.

1 Your employer sets up the account.
You set up an account with abroker of online platform.

2 Account is funded with pre-tax dollars.
Account is funded with after-tax dollars (from your savings or checking account).

3 Employer may match your contributions (extra money). No extra money is provided by your employer.

4 Employer selects plan and you tailor your investments to your needs.

**Features of a
Roth IRA**

Since your account is funded with after-tax money, withdrawals are tax-free.

You have the freedom to withdraw your contributions at any time without penalty

You get to select the brokerage firm and your individual investment options

What is a Roth 401(k)?

The Roth 401(k) is a new opportunity for many participants. It gives them the ability to use their employer sponsored plan to accumulate after tax dollars for retirement. The allowable amount is significantly higher than the traditional Roth IRA contributions that have been allowed previously. A significant difference in this is that very few plans at this point have adopted this option. Depending upon the age of the participant, the Roth 401(k) may make sense for younger people who have more time for the funds to accumulate.

Features of a Roth 401(k)	With a Roth 401(k), using a farm analogy is the easiest way to describe the features. You pay the taxes on the seed, not on the harvest.
	Those monies at distribution are tax-free.
	The rules of the Required Minimum Distribution do not apply.
	Roth 401(k)s can be transferred to beneficiaries tax-free.
	Ability to contribute more to your Roth 401(k) than was previously allowed with a typical Roth IRA.
	You are paying the taxes on the amount that is deposited rather than distributed.
	With automatic deductions, it makes participating easy.

The threshold is much higher than what was previously allowed for deposits.

It is often the case that regular folks have all of their money tied up in retirement accounts where taxes are due at distribution. As an example, I had one client who wanted to pay off his house with money from his retirement account. He didn't realize, until I pointed out, that doing so would put him in a much higher tax bracket.

Knowledge is ultimately power. Having all the facts before you make your final decisions can save you a lot of money. Making sure that there is an element of cohesiveness to your planning can and will make all of the difference in the end.

Whether you're choosing between a 401(k), a Roth IRA, a Roth 401(k), or simply trying to choose which brokerage firm you want to use to make trades and manage your investments, it's important to remember that there is never a one-size-fits-all option. To figure out what is best for you, you have to explore all of the pros and cons with each opportunity and figure out how they relate to your own situation.

The most important thing to remember is that, in most cases, time is on your side. The earlier you start investing and saving for retirement, the better off you will be. So, take time to choose which type of retirement options are best for you. But don't let having too many options deter you from making a decision altogether.

The basics of 401(k) and Roth IRA Plans:

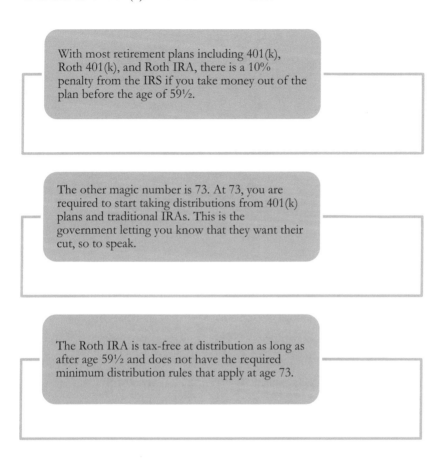

With most retirement plans including 401(k), Roth 401(k), and Roth IRA, there is a 10% penalty from the IRS if you take money out of the plan before the age of 59½.

The other magic number is 73. At 73, you are required to start taking distributions from 401(k) plans and traditional IRAs. This is the government letting you know that they want their cut, so to speak.

The Roth IRA is tax-free at distribution as long as after age 59½ and does not have the required minimum distribution rules that apply at age 73.

Consider This:
From the Desk of Dan DeVerna

A question I get asked about a lot is "Should I pay off the remainder of my mortgage?". The answer almost always is that it depends. Where the money is coming from usually determines the best approach. For instance if it comes from a traditional IRA there may be taxes owed. Whereas if the funds are coming from a Roth or a bank account we may not have that **same consideration.**

Chapter Five
How Does Social
Security Work?

When you were a kid, you probably had a piggy bank. When people gave you some change, you'd feed the piggy. One day, you decided that you needed that money, so out came your father's hammer and little piggy was busted open. At that moment, when you tallied up your money, you were probably either excited or disappointed.

With Social Security, you essentially are putting away money into a piggy bank-money you'll want for later. But many factors will decide if you are excited or disappointed when you "bust" your Social Security open to see what's inside.

If you work to your full age, you might reccive a benefit of $2,400 at age 70. But you may only receive $1,600 if you take it at age 62. So, you can see there are consequences when you break into Social Security early.

One situation that I get a lot is the I'm going to take it now while the getting is good scenario. People are always talking about getting their money out before Social Security doesn't exist anymore. The truth is that the largest demographic of the population is currently millennials rather than baby boomers. With Social Security, there are a lot of opinions on what the future of it is going to be like or whether it will even exist at all. I plan for what exists and will adapt to changes as required.

What are the basics of Social Security?

At the basic level, Social Security does two main things-it collects and distributes funds. If you work in the United States, you pay taxes into Social Security. Social Security takes that tax money and pays out benefits to those who are eligible.

Depending upon your age, you could draw out of Social Security as early as 62. At 67, you've reached what is considered your full retirement age, but you can increase your income further by deferring up to age 70. Up until your full retirement age of 66, you are restricted in the amount of income you are allowed to earn. At ages 62 to age 66, you can earn just under $19,560; then every two dollars you earn above that level, reduces your Social Security by one dollar.

Who's eligible for Social Security?

Believe it or not, Social Security is not just for retirees. Depending on your circumstances, you can be eligible to receive benefits at any age. How is that? There are four types of people who are eligible to receive Social Security benefits:

- People who've already retired
- People who are disabled
- The survivors of workers who've passed away
- The dependents of beneficiaries

When am I eligible to receive my full benefits?

Unfortunately, there isn't a simple answer. But it's not as confusing as it seems. As of 2017, if you were born between 1943 and 1960, your full retirement benefit age increases incrementally up to age 67. For fast reference, if you were born in 1950 or earlier, you are in luck. You're already eligible for your full Social Security benefit.

The chart below is from the Social Security Administration and can help you discover your full retirement age.

Birth Year	Full Retirement Age
1943 -1954	66
1955	66 and 2 months
1956	66 and 4 months
1957	66 and 6 months
1958	66 and 8 months
1959	66 and 10 months
1960 or later	67

What happens if I retire early?

Basically, you can start to collect benefits at age 62. However, the Social Security Administration will reduce those benefits if you start early to the tune of one-half of one percent for each month you begin collecting benefits prior to your full retirement age. Should your full- retirement age be 66 and two months, and you start collecting Social Security when you're 62, then you would receive just 74.2 percent of your potential full retirement benefits.

What if I delay my retirement?

Delaying when you start to receive your benefits past your full retirement age amounts to Social Security increasing your benefits by a certain percentage amount in relation to your birth year.

What do I do to apply for Social Security benefits?
When you are ready to apply for your benefits from Social Security, you can do so at their website: socialsecurity.gov/applyforbenefits.

You should plan to do this several months in advance of when you would want your benefits to begin. They may ask for certain paperwork, such as your Social Security card, birth certificate, proof of U.S. citizenship or lawful immigration status, marriage certificate, your spouse's information, any military discharge papers, and your most recent tax return.

Extra thoughts about Social Security
-People have been thinking that the program would disappear for a long time. It hasn't and probably won't. Either way, you shouldn't make decisions based on fears. Someone who does this may find themselves shortchanged.

-There are now more millennials than baby boomers, which should predict that the program will continue.

-If you are a widow, you can receive Social Security (also known as survivor's benefits) at age 60.

-If you earn income from wages or other sources, you could end up paying up to 85% taxes on your Social Security benefits.

Of course, this is a crude and rudimentary overview of some of the aspects of Social Security benefits. The truth is, Social Security benefits can be extremely confusing and complicated. And just when you think you have a handle on things, some of the rules, exceptions, and exclusions are subject to change. It's a financial professional's job to know all the details and wrinkles involved with Social Security benefits. If you have any pressing questions about Social Security and how it impacts your retirement plans, reach out to a financial professional.

The basics of Social Security
- Age based as to when you can begin receiving benefits
- Each year (until age 70) that you put off receiving benefits, your monthly amount goes up
- The amount you receive is based upon your lifelong income and the amount you paid in
- There is a maximum benefit amount
- Spousal income option with special provisions for widows and widowers
- There are cost of living increases but no guarantees on them
- You can earn some income while receiving Social Security benefits without penalty

**Consider This:
From the Desk of Dan DeVerna**

If a spouse passes away, the surviving spouse gets whichever Social Security payment is higher, **not both payments.**

Chapter Six
Affording Healthcare
in Retirement

Without good health, an integral part to a great quality of life, you have little else. Ask any dying billionaire and they'll probably give their last cent for a cure to whatever ails them. Have a heartfelt conversation with someone who has lost a spouse to illness, and to be sure, they'd have begged, borrowed, or stolen if it meant more time with the ones they loved. In the end, it is always about health and being healthy enough to enjoy life.

A friend of mine, and sufferer from smart-guy-it is, told me about the English philosopher, John Locke, who controversially published in an essay the idea that people were entitled to natural and fundamental rights. In short, these rights were life, liberty, and the pursuit of property. Think about that. Out of all the things on this earth he could select, he picked just those three. But more than that, in this highly curated list, he put life first. It would seem for John Locke, of all things, life was of the highest importance. I'm sure that when you stop to think about what truly matters, you will agree with Mr. Locke. After all, without life, not a bit of the rest of it matters.

Ever consider this common toast, "To your health!" or how about, "Salud!" Translated into English, it simply means "health". In Arab countries, it isn't uncommon to say, "Sahtein," literally meaning "two healths," before beginning a meal. But we don't have to travel far, to explicitly see the importance of health. Look no further than the continued political division in America in regards to how to handle healthcare. Health, life, and vitality are clearly important and integral aspects of our society.

We all know the importance of health and how important it is to stay in good health. But as we age, and probably grow wiser about the subject, placing a higher value on it, we are suddenly hit with the realities of the situation. Most of us will need medical care. Most of us will have prescription medications that we will come to depend upon. We will need to see doctors, and even specialists, from time to time. Some of us will need even more still. Some of us will need operations, in-home health aides, and even long-term nursing care facilities at some point. And here is the thing about all of that-we will have to have a means to pay for it.

One of the primary things to consider in retirement is how to afford healthcare costs after your career has come to an end. If you haven't been living in a cave this whole time, then you are probably aware of the exponential rate at which healthcare costs rise. When you couple that staggeringly steady cost growth with the continued increase of life expectancy, it is difficult to pin down just how much you need to save in order to match the price of healthcare as you age.

In my career, I've seen just about every possible scenario play out. Even still, new ones seem to pop up on a daily basis. The only constant is that you must be prepared for the unexpected. Because if you are not prepared, then you remove what little control you might have had from the equation.

As an example, (and I could cite you many), a client, named Jim, retired from a property and casualty insurance practice that he owned. The issue that he faced was that Jim's company held his health insurance, so when he sold his business, he lost coverage. So, from the ages of 62 to 65 he found himself paying higher premiums for his healthcare coverage under his wife's job. This also delayed the date at which his wife could retire to age 65. Basically, she had to keep working just for their health insurance needs. This is a common situation and often the number one consideration when choosing a retirement date. Besides having to be knowledgeable about certain factors, such as COBRA and the age at which Medicare kicks in, there are lots of other elements that need to be kept on your radar, no matter where in the arc of retirement planning you currently are.

Another interesting health insurance example that I want to talk about is that, in some circumstances, individuals with a lot of savings and or non-qualified investments, but little in the way of regular income, can take advantage of the subsidies provided by the government through the Healthcare Marketplace. More and more, we find ourselves advising clients to use this method. This kind of out-of-the-box thinking has helped many of our clients save substantial amounts of money.

Think about this: Many Americans over the age of 50 haven't set aside funds for their out-of-pocket medical expenses. You might be in this category. Considering that we are now regularly living past age 80, and that the amount of time we are retired is longer, and that new cutting-edge medical advances are more expensive than ever, how is it that we aren't spending more time considering squirreling away funds for health care? This is concerning!

So, in the spirit of John Locke, I've come up with three keys to consider for that all-important question about your health: How will I pay for healthcare in retirement? If this one subject seems complicated, it's because it is. Truthfully, it is extremely so. In fact, we have a full-time person focused on this specific area because of its complexities.

Don't let it raise your blood pressure though. I promise that, with a well-executed plan, you'll end up more worried about which golf club to use on that par four approach shot, rather than about how to pay for your healthcare costs. Let's try and break it down so that it is easily digested. Here we go:

What are my healthcare needs?

Individual factors like age, health, and family medical history can drastically change potential expenses. Even your list of current or potential medications is a consideration when choosing a plan.

Am I eligible for any employer-sponsored healthcare programs?

Employee benefits you receive can help offset costs and positively alter the amount you need to save for medical expenses. Learning your program options or finding a trusted professional in this area is a must if you hope to truly take advantage of and learn the intricacies of your healthcare plan and options.

Is quality health care accessible?

As you age, health care quality and costs become more important. While there is accessibility to great health care abroad, quality can vary greatly from city to city.

How much will Medicare cover?

For most retirees, Medicare is the backbone of their health care plan. But like most things over time, Medicare has gone through significant changes. There are also many supplements available to run alongside the Medicare plan. These can prove beneficial.

You know the drill. Let's take a closer look at these key questions.

What are my health care needs?

This is where you would look specifically at your individual and situational factors, such as family longevity, your current health, and your healthcare options. Then you must ask yourself-and try to answer honestly-do you get sick often? Do you go to the doctor's office frequently? How about urgent care facilities? What would you do if you had to go to the emergency room? Some of you will have a good handle on what to expect in regard to your future healthcare needs, but others won't. And the truth is that none of us have a crystal ball. We must remember that bad things happen, most times without warning. But again, having a plan in place to deal with the unexpected, as well as the expected, will almost always make a bad situation a little easier to handle for both you and your loved ones.

Am I eligible for any employer sponsored healthcare programs?

It's important to speak with a financial professional to comb over the details of your plan. The better you understand and utilize the benefits your employer has given you; the lower your total health care costs will be. Knowing specifically what your employer plan allows, and what it looks like when you retire, is extremely important. You absolutely want to have a handle on what your maximum out-of-pocket expenses could be. Of course, I say this knowing that you cannot accurately project what you will spend on unforeseen medical costs. But you may have a good idea, based on your historic needs and their costs. When looking at the details of the plan options this needs to be looked at very closely, because you may be stuck with what you pick for at least a year, even though you have the option to change plans on your anniversary date.

How much will Medicare cover?

Traditionally, Medicare parts A and B provide coverage for most needed medical visits at both the doctor's office and the hospital. You can reasonably figure on Medicare parts A and B to cover 80% of the cost. The remaining 20% of the costs will need to be paid either as an out-of-pocket expense or with Medicare supplements. Be fully aware though, this is not a hard and fast rule. In order for your Medicare to cover the 80%, the billed item must qualify as an allowable charge. As an example, elective procedures, such as cosmetic surgery, typically would not qualify as an allowable charge covered by Medicare. You can find a list of procedures and medications not covered at medicare.gov, as well as by consulting your financial professional's health care experts. They're always happy to assist you with this.

Medicare Supplements

Medicare supplements are used by many to cover or reduce the 20% of the costs not covered by Medicare alone. These Medicare supplements, or Medigap plans, as they are also known, should be discussed with your financial consultant's healthcare coverage expert, as there are many options to choose from. Not all of these options may best suit your specific needs.

What will Medicare NOT cover?

Much of your traditional hospitalization may be covered by Medicare, but as you age and need non-traditional care situations (such as an in-home health aide, a nursing home, or even hospice), you might find that those treatment options may not be covered, or at least covered much less than expected. If you are reliant on a government program to cover your needs, you will have less in the way of options, and, of course, that could make you unhappy. If you are left in a situation without much in the way of assets, most of the higher-end care facilities will have little interest in taking care of you, as they prefer a traditional premium paying resident. Also, we have seen many folks not even have the option to be in an area that is familiar to them, such as where they have grown up, or grown old, or located near family. It is often the case that someone without options or assets is relocated to a facility based on space, not location.

What alternative measures exist?

The short answer is that there are two common, but not that well-known, alternative measures. The first is traditional long-term care insurance. This is insurance that is extremely costly because of the risk that the insurance company takes on. With 50% of us needing some kind of long-term care in our lives and depending on the amount of time that the insurance company could potentially be on the hook, as well as the rising costs of healthcare in general, it is no wonder that this option isn't the most cost effective.

Traditional long-term care insurance used to be much more popular than it is now. This is because of the prohibitive costs associated with this plan. Also, another big drawback to this type of insurance is that when you die, all of the premiums are simply kept by the insurance company. It's true that you have the opportunity to buy a rider that will pass your lifetime premiums on to your heirs, but adding this feature is usually very costly. That is why most people decline this option.

The second alternative measure, which is far more typical, is the use of the newest version of life insurance. We will likely discuss this product more than once in this book because it is a tool that is like the Swiss Army knife of insurance. The newest versions of Indexed Universal Life have a hybrid option that allows, in some cases, a person that needs long-term care or has a chronic illness, to take a portion of the death benefit while they are still alive, to use for such care. This is an option that people have but are not required to execute or use at all. Most people are not familiar with this option, but we believe that it has merits.

So, now that we've covered that, let's reflect on the fact that, after life, John Locke listed liberty. In addition to the basic health costs, it's also important to think about how you will remain independent as you age. How will you remain independent if you should one day require some assistance with daily living?

In 2016, Genworth conducted a cost of care study, in part, to better determine the financial cost of a part-time home-health aide. What did they find out? Nationwide, the median cost for home-health aide services is upward of $125 a day. You don't need to be a math prodigy to figure how fast $875 bucks a week adds up. Costs can be even scarier for full-time services, like nursing home care. These are major expenditures that Medicare and employer sponsored insurance typically don't fully cover.

To help in the illustration of these points, let me tell you a story that is personal to me. You see, I grew up in Pemberville, Ohio in a 900 square foot ranch home. My dad was a welder and my mother worked for the church and at other jobs. We were part of a hard-working family. The patriarch of my family was my grandfather on my father's side. He owned and operated a towing service, so it was not uncommon for us to be at their home and watch as he had to speed off to pull someone out of a ditch. This was indeed more than just a job. It was a way of life for the DeVerna family.

The junkyard, or the "yard" as we called it, was like the Starbucks of today. The yard was where many of the local personalities would check in with my grandfather, Dolas, and the boys. In addition, my dad had his welding shop there, and my uncle and cousin both worked at the yard. Now, let's fast forward to when my grandfather became ill and passed away. At first, my grandmother moved in with us, but, in no time at all, her health deteriorated, in part, due to losing her spouse of 65 years, as well as the general wear and tear on her body from a lifetime of working. Before long, my parents could no longer care for her at our house.

She ended up having to go into a long-term care facility. The part that always gets me is that in no time at all their house and the yard, the places they had worked their whole lives for, had to be sold to pay for her care. This, in turn, had a negative impact on my uncle and cousin, as well as my father. They all worked there too.

Quickly, all of what I had known to represent my family's hard work and community building efforts was gone, sold to the highest bidder. Nowadays, it only exists as a distant memory to a few of us.

Had there been any type of preparation or planning, this could have been avoided. So, it breaks my heart that I wasn't in this line of work at the time. Maybe then, my grandfather's legacy could have been saved in some more fortunate capacity.

So, in a world where they are telling us that half of us are needing this type of care-and I think it's going to be you and you think it's going to be me-it is best to cover your bases and take care of your family and your stuff. Because no one cares more about your stuff than you do.

This is your one and only life. For your health, please start saving. Or better yet, schedule a meeting with your financial consultant today. Salud!

How do I plan for healthcare in retirement?

Explore the Marketplace at www.healthcare.gov

Know what you are offered through government programs.

Know what you are offered through employer-sponsored plans.

Know your maximum out-of-pocket costs for a year.

Pay attention to the details of medical maintenance and prescription drug costs.

Weigh out best- and worst-case scenarios annually for the programs offered.

Pay close attention to looming deadlines.

Consider This:
From the Desk of Dan DeVerna

I advise wealthier clients with money and non-qualified assets, but little in the way of income, to take advantage of subsidies provided by the government through **the Healthcare Marketplace.**

Chapter Seven
Long-Term Care Issues
and Life Insurance

In the beginning chapter of this book, I use the following quote: "Failing to plan is planning to fail". This famous wit is attributed to founding father, Benjamin Franklin. If you've spent any time in an office, there's a solid chance you've seen this quote on a motivational poster or two. But it's much more than just a quaint, glib, little saying.

When we look deeper into this line, there are two things that strike me. First, failing is easy. You don't have to do anything to fail. It's default mode. And second, is the opposite. Success is something that must be planned for. You must execute your prepared plan to fight off failure and achieve success.

If you remember Aesop's fable about the ant and the grasshopper, then you will remember that the ant toiled all summer long, preparing for winter, while the grasshopper did not. Then when winter rolled around, the grasshopper came to the ant in desperate need. The point of the story is that those who prepare for life's winter will succeed in staving off hard times, while those who choose to ignore the future's needs will fail. The same logic can certainly be applied to long-term care and life insurance.

While we tend to apply these truths to finance and preparing for natural disasters or unforeseen circumstances, I'd like for us to think about planning for health. It's something we don't like to think about. We'd like to think we'd live forever in perfect health. But, for most people reading this book, you have probably already been exposed to the realities of health issues that can occur in one's lifetime. For many of you, as well, you have lost loved ones unexpectedly. Perhaps you have even seen the consequences of death, from the standpoint of costs associated with funeral arrangements and estate issues. But, if we bury our heads in the sand and ignore planning for the future, we are guaranteeing failure. So, let's take a moment to look at long-term healthcare and life insurance, as you eye your retirement.

What are long term care issues?

Insurance companies look at a certain set of criteria, called Activities of Daily Living, when evaluating whether you qualify for using the policy. A doctor must be willing to say that you need assistance with at least two of these things:

Bathing: Getting into the tub or shower

Dressing: Putting on any necessary clothing, including undergarments and necessary braces, fasteners, or artificial limbs

Transferring: Getting into a bed, chair, or wheelchair and getting back out

Toilet: Getting to and from the toilet, getting on and off the toilet, and performing personal hygiene

Continence: Maintaining control of bowel and bladder function; or when unable, performing necessary associated hygiene, such as catheterization

Eating: Feeding yourself by getting food into your mouth from a plate or cup and being able to use utensils. When unable to feed yourself from a container, being able to feed yourself using a feeding tube.

Some simple truths to consider about the three ways to pay for long-term care:

1.   Private Pay: This is where you write the check every month out of your bank account. This scenario only works if you have the means to facilitate it for an indefinite period.

2.   Long-Term Care Insurance: This is a great planning tool but requires both foresight and money. These types of plans can be very costly because the insurance company faces a great deal of exposure financially, as long-term care is expensive, in general. Another issue to consider when buying long-term care is that, if it goes unused, the monies that you paid in premiums essentially disappear.

3.   Life Insurance with a Long-Term Care Rider: With these types of hybrid policies, at the very least, your family will get the death benefit if the long-term care benefits go unused, essentially hedging your bet. These types of policies are generally less expensive because they are based on mortality, rather than

morbidity. Also, they have a predetermined cap as to the amount that the insurance company is potentially on the hook for.

4.   Government Assistance: If you do not have either the means to comfortably pay for long-term care of either your spouse or you or both and do not hold either a long-term care insurance policy or a life insurance policy with a long-term care rider, then the government restricts the amount of assets you are allowed to keep and the amount of income you are allowed to make, forcing a "spend down" scenario.

Possible Failures	Planning Advantages
Not enough money.	Less affected by a forced "spend down" making a lifestyle change less likely.
Money but no insurance.	Having the resources to spend for long-term care.
No significant money.	Having the ability to leverage money to your advantage through planning techniques such as trusts, use of insurance, etc.

Do I really need life insurance?

You've heard this from me before, but people only get life insurance for one of two reasons-either they owe somebody, or they love somebody. Let's assume you meet one of those criteria and take a quick look at life insurance options.

Term Life Insurance

With the different basic types of term life insurance, you (a) buy a policy for a certain period of time; (b) buy it up to a certain age; or (c) have the policy as long as you work for a certain employer. The benefits are that this type of policy is inexpensive, but you are likely to outlive the policy.

Whole Life Insurance

Whole life insurance is a permanent type of life insurance with a cash value element to it. The cash value inside of the policy is tied in closely with interest rates. This was one of the original forms of life insurance, but has underperformed, due to record low interest rates. Typically, a person bought whole life insurance in the 70s or 80s when interest rates were high. They were told that not only would it act as a life insurance policy, but it could serve as a retirement plan. Now, those same people are upset because their policies have underperformed.

Universal Life Insurance

Universal life is insurance with a cash value to it. The cash value inside the policy is tied closely to the investment performance of the insurance company. These policies, although they are not performing above, or even at expectations, have far exceeded the performance of whole life contracts.

Indexed Universal Life Insurance

Another cash value life insurance policy-with this kind of life insurance, the insurance company uses an indexed account tied to different indices, such as the S&P 500. The insurance company buys options which then allows them to capture a greater upside in positive market years, while still being capped on the downside, based on contractual guarantees.

With the whole, universal, and indexed universal varieties, there exists both a ceiling and a floor that is guaranteed by contractual obligation.

Variable Universal Life Insurance

Yet another cash value life insurance policy, but rather than the investments being chosen by the insurance company, they are selected by the policy owner. These investments look much more like something you might see in your 401(k), with the possibility of being somewhat aggressive, if desired. The biggest problem with these policies is the management of volatility.

If nothing else, life insurance offers protection for you and your loved ones. Life insurance is not always the best financial investment but knowing that your loved ones will be okay financially, should something happen to you, is worth a great deal.

Knowing which type of life insurance plan is best for you and your family is not something I would expect to come naturally to you. I have been helping people with their life insurance needs for a long time and stand ready to help you navigate these confusing waters. Remember, it is your money, and you are the captain of the ship, but I can be your trusted navigator and pilot.

Passing on Life Insurance	Passing With Life Insurance
CON Exposure to Estate Taxes	PRO Tax-free income distributed to beneficiaries
CON Family Exposed to Debts	PRO Benefit paid outside of probate
CON Family Exposed to lost income	PRO Cash is provided to cover estate taxes or other debts or lost income

Sometimes decisions have to be made about circumstances that are uncomfortable. Nobody enjoys thinking about long-term care and, ultimately, death. These uncomfortable subjects should never be ignored. But there are ways to approach them without causing undue stress. I've always found that talking about them and planning for them well in advance from the neutral ground of your financial guy's office makes dealing with these things a lot easier for everyone. So, schedule an appointment today, and you can leave knowing you have a plan in place, rather than always having an uncomfortable reality lingering in the back of your head.

Long-term care & Life insurance
Many forms of life insurance now have a living benefit that can be accessed prior to death if certain qualifications are met

If correctly used, the cash value inside of a life insurance policy can be accessed on a tax-free basis, even if you have no intentions of repayment

With the increased mortality rates in people living longer than ever, the cost of insurance has never been lower

With the recent living benefits being added to certain types of life insurance, the access to cash for alternative purposes, such as long-term care, has become a bit of a Swiss Army knife

Consider This:
From the Desk of Dan DeVerna

Because most people are living longer than previous generations did, a retiree might have children that are also retirees. Often, what transpired because of this is that assets are being passed on to a generation or two below. This phenomenon is **known as "Generational Skip".**

Chapter Eight
What Should I Know
About My Retirement Plan?

Let's imagine for a moment that you're on a ski vacation. Picture yourself at the very peak of the mountain. The view from up top is spectacular. And racing down the mountain seems like a great idea, but you may want to talk to someone who has done the run to get a better idea of what lies ahead.

From this vantage point, you can choose any path down the mountain you want. But if you've never been to this resort, or let's say you don't have a trail map with you, it might behoove you to ask a local or a guide for some advice on getting down.

But what good would their advice be if they didn't know anything about you? Say you're a complete novice, but the guide sends you down a steep double black run with cliffs and rocks, because it was his favorite route. That wouldn't be much fun. Or what if they didn't know that you had a bum knee, and they send you down a slope pocked with knee-bruising moguls. Or maybe you were hoping to capture that perfect picture, but he doesn't send you toward the scenic route.

Without knowing the particulars, the details and goals, it's

difficult to have a plan or a route in place that best meets your needs. The same goes for your retirement plan. To have the best time, to get the satisfaction you want, the joy that indulges your specific and wholly individual needs, you need to know the details of your retirement plan. With that in mind, let's take a moment to consider your retirement plan before we go charging down that mountain.

These days, there seems to be a myriad of retirement plans and options out there. And the list keeps growing. It's no surprise how confusing and overwhelming this can be for the worker. Obviously, the best way to address your concerns and questions is to meet personally with a financial consultant, but in lieu of a chat, I've come up with a quick list of common retirement plan types. And, to help you navigate past the bumps and steeps you may encounter, I've provided a few special concerns you may want to think about. Let's get to it.

Major Plans	Key Components
Defined Benefit	May guarantee a lifetime retirement benefit
	Must consider factors like age, years of employment, and salary
	Largely funded by employers
	DB Plans are becoming less common
Defined Contribution	DC plans are the most popular type of employer-sponsored retirement plans
	For most people, the most common type of DC Plan is 401(k)
	You decide how much to contribute
	Employer may match contributions
Hybrid Retirement Plans	Combines features of the DB and DC Plans
	Employees may receive a stream of income or lump-sum distribution at retirement
Supplemental Retirement Plans	Allow you to save beyond what's contributed by your primary plan
	Contribution limits, early withdrawal penalties, and many details will vary
	Best to review this plan w/ a financial consultant

You know the drill. Let's take a look at these four plans in greater detail.

What is a Defined Benefit Plan?

With a Defined Benefit Plan, the employer is responsible to deliver a set amount per month to the employee or employee's spouse, typically until the entitled person is deceased. Once a promise in this situation is made, the responsible party, whether a union or an employer, is required to provide said income to the participant, and if they fail to maintain the ability to follow through on this promise, they will find themselves met with stern repercussions. In the case of the entitled person dying, benefits can be passed on to their spouse if certain criteria are in place ahead of time. As an example, a person who chooses a spousal continuation benefit could leave unto their spouse benefits for many years.

Great. So, then what's a Defined Contribution Plan?

The Defined Contribution Plan makes no promise of what you will receive. Instead, the benefactor promises what they will contribute (a certain amount) in present time to the plan and provides that the entitled individual will have access in some measure, depending upon the performance of the plan's investments, leading to a far less predictable outcome than the defined benefit plan. However, the entitled individual often has an ability to guide how what is contributed on their behalf is invested.

What should I consider with Hybrid Retirement Plans?

Hybrid Retirement Plans often allow the participant to choose the path they prefer. This allows more flexibility for the participant. Some individuals will choose an income stream without the burden of responsibility, while others choose to have more control of their investments. These types of plans offer more flexibility than either of the aforementioned types of plans.

Are there different factors to take into account with Supplemental Retirement Plans?

With Supplemental Retirement Plans, the intention is to be able to give the employee the ability to save beyond normal programs. Based upon the objective of the participant, these types of plans allow additional funding, but often are more restrictive with access to funds, while lacking flexibility.

Wait a minute. What about Social Security?

If you're confused about Social Security, trust me, you're not alone! In just the discussion of ages alone, ages 62, 67, and 70 are significant milestones, each with their own pros and cons. At age 62, most people become eligible to receive Social Security benefits but are restricted in the amount of income they can earn while receiving these benefits, should they exceed the amount allowed. There are also negative consequences that result in higher taxes and a required payback.

At 67, you are no longer restricted by how much money you can earn while drawing Social Security benefits. Every year, from age 62 to 70, that you put off collecting Social Security benefits, you receive an 8% increase in your benefits. At age 70, you no longer benefit from waiting, and, therefore, would begin to accept benefits.

It is always a good idea to refer to your financial consultant when deciding when to take the benefits, as there is a calculator that we use that can project a suitable time, based on multiple factors. In this regard, your individual situation is unique. Issues, such as personal circumstances in matters of health and family longevity history, can influence your decision for when to begin to accept benefits. As an example, if you come from a long line of octogenarians, then waiting until you were 67 to tap into the Social Security well would make sense. As a financial consultant, I have vast experience in helping people with this complicated decision.

Should I work after retiring?

More and more, I'm seeing clients retiring from work that they must do and start to work at something that they want to do. In these cases, we have very specific conversations based upon the income potential of the new career. If the new income is very insignificant, its impact on Social Security is nominal. However, as we have many people who retire and choose a pension option and then do what is referred to as double dipping, (earning a sizable income while drawing on their pension), the Social Security deferment option becomes the obvious route.

We also have many clients who pursue a consulting path which may have an inconsistent income and must be planned for accordingly. With the increase in people living longer lives, we're also seeing an increase in people who are enjoying their new lives at work. Many of my clients are looking at their retirement jobs as a new chapter. They're excited about them in the same way that they were with their apprenticeship programs so many years before.

Should I elect to use a survivor benefit option for my spouse?

Although in this area there are some personal preferences factored into the decision-making process, there are specific income maximization tools that we utilize. The instinct is to take the highest amount of income over one's life. But we've learned from experience that it is far more complicated than it appears on the surface. Doing just that might result in unintended negative consequences for your spouse, should you die before them. Therefore, since I have yet to meet an individual with a reliable crystal ball, I always like to thoroughly discuss the options for possible situations, regardless of how uncomfortable the subject matter may be.

There are options that can safeguard against leaving a loved one in the proverbial lurch. The intention here is to strike the balance between maximizing the lifetime income from our pension plan without jeopardizing the future of our family. It should be noted that almost all pension plans stop at one generation, meaning that if you are married, a spouse could potentially receive benefits from the pension if the proper measures are put in place. But, keep in mind, very rarely do the benefits ever pass on to children or grandchildren.

Do I have life insurance? Do I need life insurance?

This is one of the more popular questions that I'm asked, and I quickly steal a line from my mentor, Tim Croak. "People only buy life insurance for one of two reasons: They either owe somebody or love somebody." Although I want to agree with Tim, I have to tell you that sometimes the math just works. So, every opportunity I have, where someone else carries the risk rather than one of my clients, I seize that moment.

With the continuation of longer lifetimes for individuals, it has done something that has never been done before in the insurance world. It has lowered the cost of premiums. Part of this is based on the insurance companies being able to hold the premiums longer, and part of it is because of the increase in efficiency of these insurance products.

I often draw a parallel between a '69 Ford Bronco and a brand-new Bronco. Both are a cool way to get around town, but the newer Bronco gets better than thirty miles per gallon. With the newest insurance, you pay less in premiums and get more in benefits.

In these new hybrid policies, they not only provide significantly less expensive ways to cover risk, but they also have benefits that were previously not in existence. Benefits like long-term care or chronic illness riders are now available. This allows the individual to use these funds to pay for expenses rather than using retirement investments which often have hefty tax burdens attached.

But wait...there's more!

Some of you may be participating in a Defined Benefit Pension Plan. This allows you to participate and select from different retirement income options and schedules. As your retirement date nears, there are some crucial questions you'll want to think hard about. I've listed a few:

How much income will I need in retirement?

If there's a Deferred Retirement Option Program (DROP) available to me, is it worthwhile to continue working while my retirement benefits keep accumulating?

What other sources of income do I have?

How great is the age difference between me and my partner?

Do I have healthcare insurance options? If so, what are they?

Got time for a story? Good.

A client named James came into my office approximately five years prior to what he believed was his retirement date. We went through the money map process to chart the path for James and his wife, Janet. Through the process of wanting to maximize all of the optional benefits, we applied for life insurance on James. Now, when it came time to choose his pension options, we could answer all of his questions, laying out all of the options, allowing him to make the most informed decision.

In the process of the insurance underwriting, it was discovered that cancer was present in James' body. Although this quickly made everything else pale in the level of importance, my team quickly went to work to make amendments to James' retirement plan so James could focus on his recovery and his family, while retiring early. The point is that life can throw you an unexpected curve ball at any time. But with the right planning, you stand a better chance at not striking out.

Doing the Math. Nothing is More Important!

The reason this chapter is so important is because, when the time comes, you only get to pull the proverbial lever once in the process. Even though you may have worked for thirty years, it all comes down to one decision in the end. And you don't get a do-over if you mess it up. That is why it is so important that you come see me, or someone like me, before making the decision. You need to walk into it with all the information possible so that you can, as the old knight in Indiana Jones and the Last Crusade would say, "Choose wisely."

You will quickly realize that I'm not the only one putting such emphasis on this decision.   If you are married, you will no doubt have a bunch of signatures from people like your spouse and a notary signing off on this decision. So, if you have come to this part of the book and have still not walked through these options with a financial consultant, you need to put this book down and call me now.

Here is an example to help illustrate something that most people don't understand. Rick has the number one option of receiving $4,000 dollars a month from his pension. If he were to opt to take the whole $4,000 a month, then his wife, Nancy, would receive nothing if he died. The benefit would cease. However, if he decided to take only $3,500 a month, and if something happened to him, Nancy would then get $1,750 a month. Likewise, if he decided on taking only $3,000, then his wife would get $3,000 a month if he were to die.

Alternatively, some decide to take a lump sum. In the case of Rick, the lump sum would total $912,000. This can look sexy at face value, but you need to do the math. If you don't have the desire to pass money on to your heirs, then this option would be less than ideal. Again, it all comes down to the numbers, and, luckily for you, we can help you with the equation. Being informed when making this decision is so important, because once this decision is made, it can't be changed. You have to live with it, as do your spouse and your family.

With these questions and considerations, you'll have a better idea how to navigate down the mountain. And more importantly, if you talk to a guide, you'll be equipped to provide them with the vital information they need to better help you enjoy your journey.

What should I know about my Retirement Plan?
There is no going back once you pull the proverbial lever
You must do the math to ensure that your loved ones are taken care of
It's all in the numbers, they don't lie
A financial consultant can help you "choose wisely"

Consider This:
From the Desk of Dan DeVerna

If you take a lump sum out of a 401K or pension without it being a rollover, taxes will be withheld at a rate of at least 20% and **penalties may also apply!**

Daniel J. DeVerna

Chapter Nine
Should I Consider an
Early Retirement Package?

Story time again. When my Uncle John was 53 and was offered a package from the local utility company where he worked. It would cover his healthcare until a certain age, give him a pension option without penalty, and a lump sum distribution along with a severance package.

At 53, it seemed he was young to retire, but he was curious what his retirement options were. As we formulated the plan, it became obvious that taking the retirement package made the most sense, but the bigger question was, would John re-enter the workforce in a new fashion.

We agreed to pull the retirement lever with the caveat that we would revisit this idea of retirement on a quarterly basis. We'd see if John needed to look for other employment. While not all the stories in this book are good, this one is great. I'm pleased to report that John is now in his late sixties and never needed to re-enter the workforce. Some of this is due to his spending habits but also a result of a well thought-through plan, that although has since been modified, has proven itself to work as we always desired.

I have many success stories in my career, but this one is truly in the top ten, as this was a family member that I advised. Implementing my team's recommendations, John divested himself from some of the investments that he had been holding in his retirement plans. We found they were exposing him to unnecessary risks. The timing turned out to be exceptional, as the economy took a turn in a negative direction. I am extremely happy with my team giving this direction to the client, as it saved him from having to put restrictions on his lifestyle.

It might seem like a really easy decision that Uncle John made but understand that I presented this same scenario to four different individuals, with three of them having stellar retirements. The fourth, however, did not take my advice and decided to ride it out. I cite Warren Buffett here, who once said, "Be greedy when people are fearful, and fearful when people are greedy." John wasn't greedy, he just wanted a simple retirement, and it served him well, whereas the fourth individual swung for the fences and struck out. This is yet another example of the math being everything. You must have someone crunch the numbers with you that knows what they are doing. It truly is key to the whole decision-making process.

The "buy-out" or early retirement package is becoming increasingly popular with employers. More and more, I'm seeing companies offering their workers an early retirement. Why is that? Well, as people gain seniority, they become more expensive to the employer. The fact is that younger people just starting out in the workforce cost less to employ.

Employers typically offer you a lump-sum distribution based on a few factors; they consider things like age, your years of service, and perhaps most importantly, the finer details in your contract.

Choosing whether to accept the terms of an early retirement package is a big deal. It's a major decision. And to say it is a complex choice is an understatement. It's important to not only be informed of the details of the buy-out options, but to also consider your options and your unique circumstances. Before you make the decision to take the money and run, there are some major factors you need to think about. Lucky for you, I've got a few here to get you started.

How will early retirement affect
my pension benefits & other retirement income?
-This is data that you can receive from your employer in the offering.

Should I start taking Social Security immediately or can
I allow my benefits to grow?
- Age is a consideration with this question, along with cash flow and assets available upon retirement.

Does my buy-out come with low
or no-cost health insurance until I'm eligible to switch to
Medicare?
- This is also data that you can receive from your employer in the offering stage.
-If health insurance is excluded from this offering, you should explore the private markets before deciding.

Have I saved enough for retirement?
- Evaluation of assets accumulated, along with income sources available, as well as your desired lifestyle in retirement, helps to answer this question.

What are the tax implications of taking a lump-sum
distribution?
- Almost all lump sum distributions are allowed to remain qualified, so taxes are paid as the money is paid to the participant, rather than at the time it is transferred or rolled over.

How great is the risk of future layoffs from my employer?
- Although no one has a crystal ball, you should have a fair idea of the solvency of your employer. Also, people are often laid off by one company only to be hired in short order by another.

Do I love what I do?

- As I mentioned before and will again, we see more and more people retiring from what they must do to work at what they want to do. If you currently love what you do, then keep doing it. Money buys security and freedom but not happiness.

Right about now, you may be thinking that is a lot to digest. Let's take a closer look at these, one at a time. After all, how do you eat an elephant? Bite by bite.

How will early retirement affect my pension benefits and other retirement income?

In most instances, if your employer would like you to take an early retirement package rather than you wanting to take an early retirement package, you may be better off. However, there are obviously other circumstances, many of which cannot be planned or that can influence this and the decision on whether to take an early retirement package.

Should I start taking Social Security immediately or can I allow my benefits to grow?

This is usually based on cash flow, lifestyle, and other income sources. Unless a client has a family history of shorter lifespans, then we like to defer social security for at least a few years to maximize the benefits. We utilize a calculator, called the Social Security Analyzer, provided through Advisors Excel, that not only tells you the year you should turn on the Social Security tap, but all the way down to the specific month. The other consideration is if you happen to find a job doing something that you really love doing. The income taken from that job may cause this decision to be a no-brainer.

Does my buy-out come with low or no-cost health insurance until I'm eligible to switch to Medicare?

This is a huge consideration, as healthcare is one of the primary expenses in retirement. Unfortunately, unless they give you a program, along with the details regarding the expenses you will be paying, this is very difficult to predict. I can't tell you how many times this topic alone decided at what point someone was going to retire, and at what time to take an offered retirement package or plan.

Have I saved enough for retirement? Should I keep working to build my nest egg?

This is exactly what we cover when we walk through the money map process. We will do the math. We will take all the contents of your financial junk drawer and make sense of it. We not only want to evaluate the income streams you have, like social security, retirement savings, normal savings, assets, and properties, but we also want to look at the tax consequences from each of these income sources.

Taxes. What are the tax implications of taking a lump-sum distribution?

The initial implications of taking a lump sum distribution are nil under the assumption that you are moving the monies to an IRA or other qualified plan. Please keep in mind that these dollars are taxed when you receive the funds. So, if the money hits your bank account, understand that there will be a responsibility to pay the taxes due, either at the time of distribution or when taxes are filed the following year.

This may seem simple, but a mistake in this area can be extremely costly. I always advise assistance in this area from someone who does this every day. A misstep here could cost you.

How great is the risk of future layoffs from my employer?

Being laid off is always a risk. Employers are often eager to replace higher paid veteran staff with a younger workforce that is willing to accept lower pay. However, you should be able to have a pretty good idea as to your own job security. If not, we can look into the factors that could lead to being laid off by your employer and help you get a better level of comfort in regard to this.

How do interest rates affect your pension?

When people are looking at their pension options, they often focus on which payout is most appropriate for their situation. For instance, is it important for them to leave their spouse as a beneficiary, and, if so, to what extent? These decisions are important because when they are made, it is final. There is a large consideration that has come to light recently with the raising of interest rates by the Fed.

When it comes to lump sum payment options, as interest rates go up, the amount of money that companies are required to keep in their coffers to cover pensions goes down, which, in turn, causes the amount of your lump sum payout option to decrease.

With the swift raising of interest rates, I have seen an effect on these payments that I had never witnessed before in my career.

103

By delaying retirement, you could be sacrificing tens of thousands of dollars, while having to continue to work to recoup the loss.

Do I love what I do for a living?

For some, working brings great happiness. If you love what you do, keep at it. That old adage, love what you do and you'll never work a day in your life, is very true. So, don't feel like you need to retire at a certain age. If you are still able to fulfill your job duties and get some satisfaction from it, then putting retirement off for a while might not be a bad idea.

Clearly, there are quite a few factors that weigh-in on the decision to accept or decline a buy-out retirement package. The brief summary we went over is a great tool to start thinking about this major decision. But, with the complexities involved, speaking with a financial consultant is a great idea. Once again, I will remind you of how working on the details of retirement in a thoughtful manner helped my Joyce.

Here's a story to consider. Please keep in mind that, as people are living so much longer and living healthier lives, a successful retirement doesn't necessarily need to start at 62 or 65. Let me tell you about Tom. Tom had many options laid out to him for a traditional retirement age, including some incentives for him to leave his employer. We went through the money map process, and Tom was going to have no issues to prevent him from sailing off into the sunset of retirement. I caution you to pause-just because everyone thinks you should retire because of age or a particular package, doesn't mean you should.

What everyone is truly trying to accomplish is happiness. And what we found with Tom was that his job was very fulfilling and a big part of his identity and self-worth. The idea of Tom getting up each day without having the drive to go to work and continue what he had started seemed much less rewarding to him than the path of retirement. So, Tom, even though in his late sixties, is still working today. For him, this is his best and most purposeful retirement.

So, be careful of what influences you on making this decision. Regardless of what an advisor or family member might say, you must make this decision for yourself. Remember, once you take that package, the rules all change.

Should I consider a buy-out retirement package?

Is your employer offering you a buy-out package or are you seeking one?

What would you do if you retired early? Would it bring you greater happiness?

How would a buy-out package affect your overall retirement plan?

Consider This:
From the Desk of Dan DeVerna

Nowadays there are more and more programs to help people manage their 401ks either inside their retirement plans or externally **through financial advisors.**

Chapter Ten
Where Should I Retire?

Real estate 101. Location, location, location. Even if you don't know a thing about buying a home, you probably know that being in the right location is paramount. What's the school district like? Is it in a good neighborhood? How's the freeway access? Is there a park nearby? Location matters.

But this popular axiom also rings true when it comes to retirement. Not only when, but where to retire is an important consideration. The state, county, and city you live in can contribute to the success and happiness you find in your much deserved retirement. Unlike buying a conventional home, your retirement location requires a few special considerations.

What is the cost of living where I'll live?

Cost of living indexes factor in average expenses for transportation, food, energy, shelter, healthcare, childcare, education, and entertainment for a particular area. For instance, it is much less costly to live in Omaha, Nebraska than it is to live in San Francisco, California. When it comes to making your money stretch, it is advisable to figure in the cost of living for the area or city in which you intend to live.

Let's face it, everything seems to be getting more and more expensive these days. And if you are someone that wants to have an active retirement, doing some research into where you get the most bang for your buck while not sacrificing other favorable factors like climate, safety, and entertainment options is always a good idea. With a little effort, settling on a location that offers what you are looking for, but remains within your budget, is easily achievable. For instance, if you have lived your working years in a place that sees hard and cold winters and want to spend your retirement years in a better climate, I assure you that you can. But you might have to choose a smaller city over a large metropolitan area. For instance, there are numerous smaller and less expensive cities in Florida than Miami or Ft. Myers that still have a warm climate, proximity to the beach, and many entertainment options. The same goes for other sunny locales, like Arizona, California, and Texas.

Although there isn't an official cost of living index prepared by the U.S. government, many unofficial parties produce reports that monitor the costs of living across the United States. Comparing the national average to the area you are considering is a good idea. If the average is 100, be careful of areas that creep above a cost-of-living index over 105.

Cities with a great cost of living index:

- Memphis, Tennessee
- San Antonio, Texas
- Salt Lake City, Utah

What are the state's taxes like?

Something to consider: While states like Texas, Florida, and Alaska may have appealing broad tax plans-higher taxes, sales taxes, and increased rates for real estate may hit retirees harder. Consider states that offer breaks and incentives to retirees and seniors. Sure, most of us have heard that Texas and Florida are great states for retirees. But there are other states you may not have considered that offer great benefits. There are seven states that don't have any income tax and two more that only tax income from interest and dividends.

States with no income tax:

- Wyoming
- Florida
- Nevada
- Alaska
- Washington
- South Dakota
- Texas

States that only tax income from interest and dividends:

- New Hampshire
- Tennessee

For many of you, retiring only means leaving your current employment as you just might be looking forward to working at something else. Also, income earned from investment interest and dividends is a reality. Choosing a location in a state with favorable income tax may still be a pertinent issue.

Property tax might also be an issue to explore. If you plan on owning your home, taking an in-depth look at the most favorable states for property tax rates is a necessity.

States with the lowest property taxes in order, starting with the lowest rates:

- Louisiana
- Alabama
- West Virginia
- Arkansas
- South Carolina
- Mississippi
- New Mexico

States with the highest property taxes, in order from the highest rates:

- New Jersey
- New Hampshire
- Connecticut
- Vermont
- New York
- Rhode Island
- Illinois
- Massachusetts
- Wisconsin
- Nebraska

Taking a good look at sales tax rates can also be important. For instance, the states of Delaware, New Hampshire, and Oregon all have a 0% sales tax rate, whereas Illinois, California, and Arizona have sales tax rates over 10%. Exploring how a given state's sales tax rates could influence your budget is something that a good financial consultant can help you with. And the same goes for the other types of taxes and what kinds of effects they can have on your retirement.

How robust is the economy?

If you have ever studied the natural world, then you know that the health of an ecosystem is very important. You will also know that there are many factors that play a role in determining whether the ecosystem is healthy. Think of where you live or might want to live as an ecosystem, as well. Economic factors can have a huge effect on the overall health of a given location. If unemployment is high, then crime rates are generally high, which, in turn, influences the prospects for your safety. You most likely want to look for an area that has a better unemployment rate than the national average. Strong economies typically hold better housing prices and promote safer living. They also offer more in the way of entertainment options, are more conducive to healthy living, and promote a better overall quality of life.

Areas with prolonged and sustained strong economies:
- Fort Collins, Colorado
- Salt Lake City, Utah
- Charleston, South Carolina
- Cedar Rapids, Iowa

Do I have comfortable access to good healthcare?

As you age, access and availability to good healthcare becomes more and more important. Some places are much better than others when it comes to healthcare. Even more to the point, some places are downright scary when it comes to their lack of physicians and healthcare facilities. One good way to measure a location's healthcare facilities is by the number of physicians per capita.

Cities with a high physician's per capita rate:

- Saline, Michigan
- Blowing Rock, North Carolina
- Cherokee, North Carolina
- Dillingham, Alaska
- Wrangell, Alaska
- Livermore, California
- Anson, Texas
- Petersburg, Alaska

How safe is the neighborhood?

Let's face it, nobody wants to live in a place where they don't feel safe. Additionally, safer neighborhoods, and, in general, cities with lower violent crime rates, maintain higher property values and better quality of life. So, if relocating is on your radar, do a little research into crime rates for all of your prospective destinations. Here are a few examples of cities with low violent crime rates. You can do a more thorough search on the FBI's website, FBI.gov.

Cities with low violent crime rates:

- Cape Coral, Florida
- Honolulu, Hawaii
- Bellevue, Washington

Does my neighborhood and community promote good health?

Consider things like walking and biking, or fair weather, that promotes you to maintain an active lifestyle. Websites like redfin.com allow you to quickly search how your city fares at being walkable and transit friendly. Are there farmers markets, shops, and errands you can run on foot? These activities can help promote a longer and healthier life. Obviously, bigger cities will have the best walkability scores. New York, San Francisco, and Boston typically top the charts, year after year. But there are some other cities that may surprise you with their pedestrian friendliness.

More cities with high walking scores:

- St. Louis, Missouri
- Rochester, New York
- Providence, Rhode Island

A quick internet search can instantly field you a list of places to retire. Hopefully the questions we asked here can help you better navigate which city best fits your needs. So, whether you imagine yourself in the outdoor activity capital of Boulder, Colorado, or in a sleepy beach town in the Carolinas, or somewhere completely different from both of those, the point is, America offers a vast array of options. Just make sure to do your homework and prioritize the qualities a place to live in has that are most important to you.

Where Should I Retire?

Consider these qualities when selecting your retirement locale:

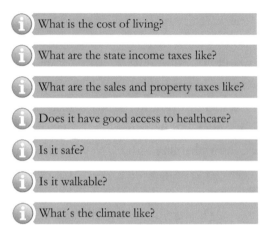

What is the cost of living?

What are the state income taxes like?

What are the sales and property taxes like?

Does it have good access to healthcare?

Is it safe?

Is it walkable?

What's the climate like?

Let's finish up this chapter with a bit of fun and fast facts about some of my clients' favorite destination retirement living spots. The concept of destination retirement living is not new but may be new to you. Basically, it involves relocating either permanently or semi-permanently to a place that you may already love to visit on vacation. As well, the places that I consider excellent choices for destination retirement living typically welcome retirees with open arms through excellent healthcare, warm or mild climates, low taxes, and a plethora of activities designed to make your golden years both fun and active.

We'll start with the obvious choice: Florida. In the Sunshine State, you will, of course, find great year-round weather, as well as the above-mentioned factors, like tax benefits, activities, and great healthcare. It really is a paradise for retirees, and, as an extra bonus, I guarantee that if you choose to make Florida your destination retirement living spot, you will never be short of family and friends wanting to come visit.

First, I am going to highlight some of my favorite cities, and then I am going to take a deeper dive into the most well-known retirement community in the country: The Villages. So, let's get started.

Fun and Fast Facts
Florida and The Villages

Vero Beach

- ☐ Beautiful community located midway down Florida's East Coast
- ☐ Smaller population
- ☐ Village atmosphere
- ☐ World class arts and culture venues
- ☐ Historic downtown loaded with shopping, parks, and restaurants
- ☐ Fantastic golf courses
- ☐ Watersports and fishing
- ☐ Resort style retirement communities

Sarasota

- ☐ Gorgeous Gulf Coast community
- ☐ Known for its great beaches, like Siesta Key
- ☐ Many attractions, like the opera house, art galleries, and aquarium
- ☐ Variety of fantastic housing options
- ☐ World renowned golf courses
- ☐ Active tennis community
- ☐ Excellent job market

Punta Gorda

- ☐ Located on the Gulf Coast between Sarasota and Fort Myers
- ☐ Beautiful waterfront community
- ☐ Small town feel chock full of natural beauty
- ☐ Often ranked in top ten places to retire
- ☐ Very affordable cost of living and median home prices
- ☐ Check out the Wine and Jazz Festival
- ☐ Home to 'Fisherman's Village' which boasts a great offering of restaurants
- ☐ Situated on Charlotte's Harbor makes it a haven for boaters
- ☐ Plenty of great golf courses

Melbourne

- ☐ Hub of the booming 'Space Coast'
- ☐ Home to Kennedy Space Center at Cape Canaveral
- ☐ Soft white sand beaches
- ☐ Fun downtown with plenty of restaurants, cafes, and shopping
- ☐ Many municipal golf courses
- ☐ Museums and performing arts centers offer cultural getaways
- ☐ Situated midway on Florida's East Coast
- ☐ Affordable beach retirement location

Ormond Beach

- ☐ Attractive for its low cost of living
- ☐ Neighbor city to Daytona means motorsports enthusiasts love it
- ☐ Museums, gardens, and lots of entertainment
- ☐ Small town feel
- ☐ Hiking trails abound at nearby state parks
- ☐ Kayak the Tomoka River
- ☐ Short drive to Orlando or historic St. Augustine

Winter Haven

- ☐ Central Florida location means entertainment and activities are always close by
- ☐ Near Orlando area attractions, such as Disney, Universal Studios, and SeaWorld
- ☐ Just 90 minutes by car to both Atlantic and Gulf Coast Beaches
- ☐ Quiet oasis nestled in the heart of action
- ☐ Easy access to over 55 lakes make it a watersports enthusiasts' paradise
- ☐ Excellent year-round climate for outdoor activities
- ☐ Virtually impossible to be without something to do
- ☐ Great restaurants, nightlife, and world class entertainment on your doorstep

Fort Myers

- ☐ Gem of Southwest Florida
- ☐ Just a short drive to Southwest Florida International Airport
- ☐ Scenic Gulf Coast views
- ☐ Just North of Bustling Naples
- ☐ Situated on the Caloosahatchee River
- ☐ Close to Captiva, Sanibel Island, and Pine Island resort destinations
- ☐ Plenty of activities, like golfing and fishing
- ☐ Loaded with great restaurants, shopping, and performing arts

Now that we have covered most of my favorite cities in Florida, let's go over the skinny on a real retirement gem: The Villages.

The Villages is known as America's best retirement community, with more than 125,000 people calling it home. Started in the 1960's by a businessman from Michigan, The Villages has grown to become the premier retirement community in all of Florida, if not all of the United States. Here are some fast and fun facts about The Villages.

The Villages

- ☐ Average age of residents is 69
- ☐ Largest Retirement Community in the World
- ☐ Approximately 32 Square Miles with 17 districts throughout 3 counties

- ☐ Residents must be at least 55 years old
- ☐ Children and grandchildren are welcome, however those under 19 years old can only stay 30 days
- ☐ Home and Villa options start around $150,000 and go up from there
- ☐ Most residents get around using golf carts, many of which have been customized
- ☐ In fact, there are over 65,000 golf carts in The Villages
- ☐ Residents can choose to live there seasonally or all year round
- ☐ Excellent security makes the Villages a very safe community
- ☐ Three Town Squares with free performances and multi-screen theaters
- ☐ Dine at an almost infinite selection of restaurants, cafes, and bars
- ☐ Endless shopping possibilities
- ☐ Access to world class healthcare facilities
- ☐ Golfer's paradise with 38 Executive Courses and 12 Championship Courses
- ☐ Over 2,500 clubs, from Birdwatching to Ballroom Dance from Target Practice to Tennis
- ☐ Live entertainment every single day of the year
- ☐ Eleven softball fields
- ☐ Over 80 swimming pools
- ☐ More than 100 recreational centers
- ☐ Besides having a club for just about everyone, there is also a Learning College

Of course, Florida is great, but it isn't necessarily everyone's cup of tea. Some of you may prefer a retirement destination with a milder seasonal climate. For this, I don't think you can beat North Carolina. With hot summers and mild winters, North Carolina offers the retiree a friendly environment, boasting low taxes, a lower cost of living, affordable housing, and excellent healthcare. Let's look now at some of my favorite spots in North Carolina.

Fun and Fast Facts
North Carolina

Charlotte, N.C.

- ☐ Largest city in North Carolina
- ☐ Old-fashioned southern charm is abundant
- ☐ Top-notch culinary scene
- ☐ Close proximity to Asheville and the Smokey Mountains
- ☐ Numerous 55+ Senior communities
- ☐ Major international airport

Piedmont Region, N.C.

- ☐ Home to Raleigh, Durham, and Chapel Hill (The Research Triangle)
- ☐ North Carolina state capital
- ☐ Tons of outdoor activities
- ☐ World-renowned healthcare facilities
- ☐ College town vibes

Asheville, N.C.

- ☐ Nestled in the scenic Blue Ridge Mountains
- ☐ Small town feel with a population of approximately 75,000
- ☐ Mild weather all year round
- ☐ Stunning picturesque scenery
- ☐ Home to the Biltmore Estate, America's largest private residence
- ☐ Hip downtown loaded with Art Deco architecture
- ☐ Many antique stores, chic boutiques, and galleries
- ☐ Excellent dining, as well as cafes, coffee shops, and tea houses
- ☐ Funky art and music scene
- ☐ Land of outdoor adventures

Wilmington

- ☐ Outer Banks location makes it a beachcomber's paradise
- ☐ Great for fishing and watersports
- ☐ Historic port
- ☐ Dog-welcoming downtown
- ☐ Designed for those who like it laid back
- ☐ Shop local at one of the many small shops and boutiques

If Florida and North Carolina just aren't big enough, no worries. Everything is bigger in Texas, so the saying goes. The truth is, it's no surprise that Texas remains a popular retirement destination. With a favorable tax code, favorable cost of living, and favorable weather, it's easy to see why the Lonestar State is many retirees' favorite spot to hang their "Ten Gallon Hat". With over 600 hospitals, and consistently ranking as an affordable healthcare haven, Texas has a lot to like. Let's look now at some of my recommendations on where to tie up your horse!

Texas
Fun and Fast Facts

Austin
- [ ] State capitol
- [ ] Home to live music galore
- [ ] Lives by the slogan "Keep Austin Weird"
- [ ] Loaded with golf courses
- [ ] Sophisticated culinary scene
- [ ] Nightlife is never in short supply
- [ ] Excellent healthcare
- [ ] A lot of bang for your buck

San Antonio

- ☐ A fast-growing population that is known as the happiest in the country
- ☐ Warm weather
- ☐ Big city offerings with small town vibe
- ☐ Dynamic downtown known as Riverwalk
- ☐ Professional basketball team
- ☐ Excellent place for those on a budget
- ☐ World-class healthcare facilities

Dallas/Fort Worth

- ☐ If access to healthcare is a priority look no further
- ☐ Home to Baylor University Medical Center and UT Southwestern Medical Center
- ☐ All of the trappings of a major U.S. city are here
- ☐ International airport
- ☐ Vibrant nightlife
- ☐ Dining for every taste
- ☐ Arts and culture offerings
- ☐ Professional sports teams

Houston

- ☐ America's 4th largest city
- ☐ Proximity to Gulf of Mexico beach areas
- ☐ University town
- ☐ The other space race location
- ☐ Culture and music abound
- ☐ Restaurant and bar scene is out of this world
- ☐ Lots of great golf courses

If being tied down to one location isn't your idea of a great retirement, maybe you should consider the RV Lifestyle. Recreational vehicles have come a long way in terms of their design, sophistication, and offerings. As well, RV resorts are becoming ever more abundant and increasingly opulent. A typical modern RV resort is nothing like an ordinary campground that you might remember from your childhood. Nowadays they offer exclusivity, boundless amenities, and unmatched experiences.

But the best part about the RV lifestyle trend is that, if you get bored and yearn for something different, all that you must do is pack up and drive off. The United States is blessed with a wide variety of national and state parks just waiting to be your temporary home. On a budget or looking for more solitude? Try parking lot surfing or boondocking on federal land. This sort of off-grid camping is free! But before you go let's go over some basics.

RV Lifestyle
Fun and Fast Facts

Motorhomes Class A
- ☐ Class A are big, up to 45 feet long
- ☐ Often have expanding pop-out technology to boost your living area
- ☐ Easily pull behind a car, motorcycles, or boats

☐ Wide range of amenities and décor available

☐ High price tag, but if it's your main residence, easily j justifiable

Motorhomes Class B

☐ Smaller van-based design

☐ Perfect for couples

☐ Small enough to explore urban areas

☐ More affordable to purchase, own, and operate than their bigger cousins

☐ Offerings include your more basic options to opulent and luxurious

☐ Off-road versions available

Motorhomes Class C

☐ Midsized for those who want something more than a B, but not an A

☐ A lot of bang for your buck when it comes to living space and amenities

☐ Towing capable

☐ Comfortable

☐ Drives like a standard truck

Towable Trailers

☐ Available in many sizes and lengths

☐ Choose your level of luxury

☐ Pop-out technology adds living space

☐ Unhook your tow vehicle to be more mobile

☐ Ultralight models available that can be towed with smaller vehicles

Fifth Wheel Trailers

☐ Gooseneck connection makes them easier to maneuver and gives extra space
☐ Must have the right kind of tow vehicle
☐ Pop-out technology adds extra living space
☐ Wide range of amenities means you can make your RV as luxurious as you can afford
☐ Park, unhook, and go explore

When it comes to Destination Retirement Living, I have a lot to say. Sure, I've written a book on the subject, as well as a few articles, and the truth is, I'm working on another book on Retirement Destinations, but if you really want to explore all your options, reach out to me. I'd be happy to help you figure out where you want to be and how you're going to get there. Let's call it a passion of mine.

Chapter Eleven
Can I Retire Abroad?

As of 2023, the Social Security Administration states that just under 450,000 American retirees are now living abroad. Most often, the countries they are moving to are Japan, Canada, Mexico, the United Kingdom, and Germany.

The rationale most retirees give for moving beyond the U.S. borders is cost of living. In many cases, beach cities outside the United States can stretch your dollar. But there's a great big world out there. Let's look at a few questions to ask if you should think about retiring abroad. And, for a little fun, let's think about some places you may not have considered for that exotic place to retire.

Will there be a language barrier?

Most of the world speaks some English and there is more affordable access to robust language curriculum than ever before.

Can I integrate with the local culture?

As an expatriate, you can expect to feel some isolation in a new community. Spend a few months in the area before you move and consider areas with more expatriates. Energetic communities can aid in feeling more a part of the culture.

Is quality health care accessible?

As you age, health care quality and costs become more important. While there is accessibility to great health care abroad, quality can vary greatly from city to city.

What's the cost-of-living difference?

Talk to your financial consultant to discuss how living abroad can affect your portfolio. Don't forget to add up relocation costs, furnishings, utilities, and amenities when comparing your domestic and foreign budgets.

Are there any tax advantages abroad?

Remember, the IRS taxes U.S. citizens on their income no matter where they live although some countries offer tax treaties.

Will there be a language barrier?

English is widely spoken around the world, but still, language can be a barrier to living the best quality of life when abroad. Many places have large expat communities, where the English language is very common, sometimes even more prevalently spoken than the native language. In many communities like southern Spain, coastal Portugal, and throughout Costa Rica and Panama, English speaking expat communities thrive.

For those of you looking to get more immersed, wanting to live like a local, there are numerous ways to learn a second language. With an abundance of language learning courses, tutors, community college offerings, and even free language learning apps on your phone, don't be scared off by the thought of having to learn a foreign language. I'm sure many of you would find it to be an exciting challenge, where the rewards are exotic locales, tropical beaches, and cosmopolitan culture capitals.

Countries with high English-speaking populations:

- Canada
- Australia
- New Zealand
- United Kingdom
- Italy
- Spain
- Brazil

Can I integrate with the local culture?

The answer to this question depends on your mentality and the culture of the place you are considering. Western-minded countries like those in the Caribbean, Western Europe, as well as Australia, New Zealand, and Canada, are all pretty close in values and laws to what you are used to in the United States. Latin American countries can be great on the cost-of-living index, but there definitely exists a difference in culture and established legal systems.

Less popular locations can be found in Asia, Africa, and the Middle East. Some of these places, such as Thailand, have very interesting offerings for retirees, like VIP residency programs. These programs come with many perks, including a concierge to handle all kinds of needs, like cutting through red tape. Choosing a more exotic location depends on your interest level. But, for a few of you, relocating to somewhere exotic that stretches your dollar might be something you are keen to do.

Obviously, Canada, Mexico, and Europe are popular destinations. Here are a few more that Americans are moving to in retirement.

Countries with higher U.S. expatriate populations:

- Israel
- Brazil
- The Philippines
- Dominican Republic
- Japan
- Colombia
- China and Hong Kong

Do I have comfortable access to good healthcare?

Once again, a great measure to go by is physicians per capita. Many countries can have variance in the quality of healthcare from city to city. If you require specialty care, you may need to budget for travel and extended lodging.

Foreign countries with robust healthcare systems:

- Sweden
- Denmark
- Netherlands
- United Kingdom
- Canada
- New Zealand
- Austria
- Australia
- Uruguay

What's the cost-of-living difference?

Some of the factors that have to be considered, in budgeting a true cost of living difference between living abroad and living in the United States, are things like cell phone plans, cable, utilities, and groceries. These factors can be wildly expensive compared to domestic rates. Consider the cost of moving. As you know, moving is much more than just getting a place. How will you furnish it? Will you be driving? These things can add up in a hurry.

Beachfront countries with lower cost of living:
- Thailand
- Portugal
- Panama
- Belize
- Malaysia

What are the tax advantages to living abroad?

The IRS taxes U.S. Citizens no matter where they live. In most instances, you are expected to file an income tax return, even if you live in a tax-free country, like the Cayman Islands. Some countries offer tax treaties with the United States which help you avoid being double taxed. Many more places offer treaties than just Canada and Mexico.

Countries with U.S. tax treaties:
- South Africa
- Japan
- Venezuela
- Barbados
- Italy
- Iceland
- Israel

I urge you to consult with a financial consultant or tax advisor to discuss portfolio and tax implications in regard to the countries you may be considering.

As I've said before, it's never too early to dream. And it never hurts to explore what your options are, even if you never end up using them. To get you started with your dreaming, here are five cities that might satisfy your thirst for adventure and romance.

Five cities for retiring abroad:

1. Algarve, Portugal

With a great climate, large expat community, and beautiful beaches, this city ranks high on just about everyone's list for retiring abroad.

2. Las Terrenas, Dominican Republic

What do you think about white sand beaches and French restaurants? I think it sounds amazing.

3. Pau, France

Located in the southwestern Basque area of France, near the Spanish border, this area is the type of lush French countryside that retirement dreams are made of. Perhaps that is why so many Brits have been calling it home for such a long time.

4. Chiang Mai, Thailand

How would you like to live like the King and Queen of Siam on just $1,100 a month? Well, in the history rich, exotic, and bustling international city of Chiang Mai, you can do just that.

5. Playa del Carmen, México

If turquoise Caribbean waters, beautiful beaches, and great scuba diving sounds appealing, then Playa del Carmen might just be the spot for you. It already hosts a large expat community, making integration into the area even easier for newcomers.

Is retiring outside the U.S. right for me?

The cost of living abroad can be considerably less than in the U.S.

A strong U.S. dollar can get you much more bang for your buck.

Vibrant cities, beautiful beach towns, and culture abound in many locations.

Language can be a barrier but can be overcome.

Healthcare is always an issue to research thoroughly, but oftentimes, you can receive first-world care at a vast discount.

Explore tax implications with your financial consultant.

Chapter Twelve
How Can a Financial
Professional Help Me Retire?

In the first versions of this book, I started this chapter off with a story about preparing for bringing children into this world. But, as with all of us, things evolve over time. Hence the title of the first chapter in this new book, 'Evolution'. It doesn't seem that long ago that I was doing that with my children. Building nurseries, changing diapers, and the rest. But, since then, and more importantly since the writing of that first book, I have witnessed my son Drake finishing his time with the U.S. Navy and starting a new life pursuing his passion for comedy in Chicago. Meanwhile, my daughter Chloe graduated from high school and started her collegiate endeavors at Ohio University in Athens, Ohio. And my son Brody is nearing his graduation from high school and all the while has been transitioning from a boy to a young man.

So, instead of talking about swaddling blankets and nervously expecting your baby to enter the world and change your life, this chapter has evolved into nervously watching your children leave the nest. That's life. That's evolution. And for the purposes of this book, it is now the parable by which we will lead into our discussion on preparation.

You see, preparing for that day when your child leaves the nest for their next chapter of life can come quickly and be daunting. I wasn't so much worried about my two sons, but my daughter, my little girl, going off to college did provide me with some sleepless nights.

Planning for retirement can do the same thing to your peaceful slumbering. Sure, it's exciting to think about, but let's be honest, it's a little scary too. For many of you, going to your career has been more than just a job or a routine. It's been part of your identity, who you are so to speak. Also, your coworkers may have become your second family or at the very least friends. Then there is the other, possibly more daunting facet to retirement, the money aspect. Will you have enough, did you plan well? How will you afford healthcare in retirement, and of course the question of will you be able to do all of the things that you dreamed of doing in retirement while you were still working? And so many other concerns.

As I said earlier, you don't buy a dog and bark yourself. Chances are that you are not by trade or education, a financial consultant with years of experience in retirement planning, investing, and managing wealth. It's also probably true to say that financial planning isn't your passion, and your idea of a good time is not going to seminars to listen to economists. For that last one I can't say that I blame you, it takes a special breed to enjoy those sorts of talks. But, luckily for you, like any financial planner worth their weight in salt, I do enjoy those things. I am in fact passionate about investing, wealth management, and the ins and outs of retirement planning. Aside from Jiu Jitsu practice, it is what gives me that rush that we all are looking for in some form.

The same goes for your retirement. Odds are, you have never planned for your retirement before. It's a big day. Sure, you've probably gotten some advice from those who've gone through it before, but for a financial consultant who focuses on retirement planning, they have the strategies, tips, and advice you can count on to make sure your dreams are fully realized.

Before we push ahead, let's look at a few ways a financial consultant can help you retire.

What financial guidance have you had up until now?

For many people, an experience like this might seem familiar. You've had someone managing your 401(k) and/or other assets. Maybe you speak to them often or maybe you've left the heavy lifting of decision-making up to them. Perhaps you have only met for donuts and coffee on the odd occasion, with no real advice given.

Yet, for others of you, perhaps you are the do-it-yourself type, and have grabbed the bull by the horns and managed everything all alone. No matter what your experience with financial guidance has been, the reality is this. As retirement nears, the gravity of the situation becomes much more significant.

People in their younger years are typically more worried about outperforming the market. But as you get to the retirement stage, the rate of return takes on less importance. It's the quality of the plan that becomes paramount. Not many people feel comfortable pulling the retirement lever without the knowledge that the ever-important math has truly been done.

Although I have met some people capable of crunching these numbers, my recommendation is always to meet with someone who focuses on this type of financial planning and does it as their primary occupation. Frankly, there are a lot of moving parts to grapple with.

What's my retirement strategy?

I can't stress enough the importance of a good retirement plan. This is the rest of your life. Why would you just wing it? Financial consultants can look at your unique needs and situation and develop a strategy and plan that is tailored to you.

Whether you consider yourself an aggressive or a conservative investor, it is always advisable to have a great strategy. Unless you're in the upper stratosphere of wealth, you are going to need a plan to adhere to. For most of us, we fall into a category closer to the middle of the spectrum where our needs are not completely met by the State and likewise, we are not so well off that we can do whatever we want without financial consequences.

Good planning can mean the difference between an uncertain fate or one where choices are positive in nature, and we are the ones choosing them. Obviously, there are always situations that can arise beyond our control. But don't let these fears prevent you from formulating a sound plan for your retirement.

What kind of guidance do I have for retirement?

Let me give you an example. A client walked in after having used an online tool to determine his options and his best way forward. The problem was that he had made some mistakes and some poor assumptions.

For one, he used a number for his rate of return on his investments that didn't accurately calculate the whole story of the market's performance. For example, when the market was down, way down in 2007 and 2008, it had a major effect on the overall strength of a portfolio over time.

Now, as much as we would all like to pretend like that crisis never took place, it did. If you don't include occurrences like that into your plan, you'll be making the same kinds of poor assumptions that this gentleman made. My advice is always to plan thoroughly, to be honest in your planning, and to seek help from someone who deals with these types of things every day.

But it doesn't end there. This same client made other poor assumptions when working with the online tool. He assumed that he knew when and how often he would need a new vehicle, and even scarier, he thought that he could predict when he would need long term care. I assure you that had he been able to correctly predict this, I would have hired him on the spot!

Another caution to think about when using online software tools, is that they usually don't have inflation factored in, or any guidance on Social Security and what year that should be turned on, and almost never will you see a pension calculator.

Am I protected from the unknown?

One of the unique parts of working with someone who does this every day is that they see things that you could not possibly even know how to look for. When it comes to retirement planning, the real pitfall (that will seem painfully obvious once I've said it) is that you don't want to be in a position where running out of money is possible.

When you work with someone who focuses on retirement planning, rather than someone whose endeavor is to maximize the biggest possible ROI, differences in strategy go hand-in-hand, with the fact that the end goals are not the same.

Likewise, in this modern world, you can find advice on how to do everything with a Google search or by watching a two-minute YouTube video. But you wouldn't necessarily set out to climb Mt. Everest after watching an instructional video some guy made in his basement, would you? Well, let's hope that you put that same sort of weight in the decision making when it comes to the guide leading you to the summit of your retirement.

I mean that, one way or another, you are paying for the guidance, so make sure that your guide has the same goals in mind 3as you. More importantly, be certain that your guide fully realizes what your goals really are. It is all too easy to get swept up in risky plays. But remember this. It is the sexy maneuvers that often help you cross the finish line.

There is an immense amount of importance when preparing for the unexpected pitfalls of life. An experienced financial consultant, especially one focused on retirement planning, can help you be best prepared to conquer what lies ahead.

While it may be uncomfortable to address, it's crucial to ensure our loved ones and family are taken care of in our absence. A financial consultant can help you set up a legacy for your family.

I have had experience with people failing to change their beneficiaries, leaving their estates to the wrong person. In today's world, second and third marriages are commonplace. An atmosphere of his, hers, and theirs kind of thinking exists. This can complicate things. And in my experience, it becomes less of an issue if addressed by a financial consultant in a professional atmosphere, rather than being tackled at the breakfast table.

In the world we live in these days, it is very common for couples to have children from previous relationships. This can complicate matters and become very uncomfortable. Worse still, is that if these types of issues are not planned for in advance, the loved ones left behind can have real problems. Planning for all of these types of issues with a financial consultant can save a lot of unnecessary trouble.

So, just like you sought advice from doctors, nurses, midwives, Mom, and probably a lot of books before you brought your baby home, the same logic should be applied to bringing the baby of your retirement plan home. And, just like how you didn't do the first life experience all alone, you don't want to try to plan for such an important milestone in life alone.

Don't worry. You don't have to think about your retirement alone. My team and I are here to guide you every step of the way. We are here for all those hard decisions, the uncomfortable moments, the dreaming, the planning, the execution, and the point at which you pull that proverbial lever and cross the finish line. We'll even be here to help you beyond that moment. I promise that no matter what, we'll make the process as easy and rewarding as possible so that you can have the potential to live your dream retirement to its maximum capacity.

How can a financial consultant help me retire?

With a financial consultant, you will have access to an array of specialized tools like:

And a whole team of professionals is devoted to your retirement's success.

Consider This:
From the Desk of Dan DeVerna

The year 2022 was the worst year for 'Modern Portfolio Theory' in the last 100 years. This was because of the poor performance of the Nasdaq, S & P 500, and the Bond Market. This is one reason that working with a financial advisor can give you an advantage over using an age based **"DIY" portfolio plan.**

Chapter Thirteen
Retirement is Just
the Beginning...

Hey, look at you! You made it to the end of yet another one of my books. I'm impressed! Afterall I am a financial consultant, not a professional author. Still, you are here, which means you've gotten to know me a little bit better while learning about some pretty boring but necessary stuff like different types of plans, tax codes, and healthcare and insurance. To keep your attention, I did go over some of the more interesting things like retirement destinations, alternative retirement lifestyles, and even where you can go abroad to stretch your dollars.

If you've been a client of mine for a while, it probably means that this is at least the second time you're reading a version of this book. Although, this is a new, improved, and evolved version. But even though you have evolved, and I have evolved and the laws and the world have both evolved, one thing remains as true today as the day that I wrote that first page of the first version of this book back in 2016, hard work, smart planning, and a little imagination, are the ingredients for a great retirement.

What exactly does the title of this book mean? Well, probably something a bit different for all of us, although I'm sure that the underlying message is the same for everyone. How retirement looks depends on what your goals are. What your dreams are. Where you go. And what you do. Remember those clients of mine with the sailboat? Well, I've been following along on their adventures by email and on their Instagram posts, and I have got to tell you that they are indeed living their dream retirement and for them it is only getting started.

Your own retirement journey, that is to say, when the day comes, and you pull the proverbial lever will be uniquely yours. For some it will mean travel, while for others, relaxation. Either way, whether you are more or less active, I'm sure you will spend a lot of quality time with friends and family. Some of you will work at other endeavors, maybe start a business or volunteer, both of which are typically very rewarding. In any case, your time will be yours. Yours to do with as you see fit. And if you're anything like me, you understand the value of that. The value of time. In fact, it is probably one of, if not the most, important assets any of us have.

In this book, I talk a lot about the financial preparations needed to retire well. And yes, they are numerous. A great retirement takes planning, preparation, sacrifice, and benefits greatly from good advice from a trustworthy professional.

Earlier I spoke about a passion of mine. Brazilian Jiu Jitsu, which I described as a contest of physical chess. Financial planning at times can be very similar. As the world evolves and the market forces change you must be thinking a few moves ahead. While at the same time, be ready to change up your tactics in an instant, because there is no pause button in life. As I wrote in the first chapter, life comes at you hard and fast, and what is today, most likely, will not be tomorrow. But that's okay, because while you've been working your financial consultant has been making sure that your money is hard at work too!

In the end, whether you are just starting your career and your retirement planning or finishing up your last years of hard work and service or somewhere in between, you have a lot to look forward to. I have been doing this job for a long time and I have to say that I love it more and more as time goes by. I love getting to know my clients, getting to watch their lives evolve, and most importantly, I love the fact that I get to help folks just like you retire well knowing that the fruits of their labor will be sweet and bountiful. I love getting postcards from clients who have taken that dream trip or moved to that retirement destination. So, if you haven't already, bring your financial junk drawer and come dump it on my desk. Because I love nothing more than meeting strangers for the first time, watching them turn into friends, and seeing for myself that 'Retirement is Just the Beginning'!

Made in the USA
Columbia, SC
29 October 2024